OTHER BOOKS BY CATHIE KATZ

The Nature of Florida's Ocean Life

The Nature of Florida's Neighborhoods

The Nature of Florida's Waterways

The Nature of Florida's Beaches

NATURE

a Day at a Time

NATURE
a Day at a Time

An Uncommon Look at Common Wildlife

Cathie Katz

Sierra Club Books · San Francisco

The Sierra Club, founded in 1892 by John Muir, has devoted itself to the study and protection of the earth's scenic and ecological resources—mountains, wetlands, woodlands, wild shores and rivers, deserts and plains. The publishing program of the Sierra Club offers books to the public as a nonprofit educational service in the hope that they may enlarge the public's understanding of the Club's basic concerns. The point of view expressed in each book, however, does not necessarily represent that of the Club. The Sierra Club has some sixty chapters coast to coast, in Canada, Hawaii, and Alaska. For information about how you may participate in its programs to preserve wilderness and the quality of life, please address inquiries to Sierra Club, 85 Second Street, San Francisco, CA 94105.

www.sierraclub.org/books

Published by Sierra Club Books, in conjunction with Random House, Inc.

Owing to limitations of space, acknowledgments of permission to quote from previously published materials will be found following the text.

Library of Congress Cataloging-in-Publication Data
Katz, Cathie.
Nature a day at a time: an uncommon look at common wildlife / by Cathie Katz.
p.   cm.
ISBN 1-57805-050-2 (alk. paper)
1. Natural history. 2. Nature. 3. Human behavior. I. Title.

QH82 .K38 2000   508—dc21   99-086436

Book design by Caroline Cunningham
Illustrations by Cathie Katz
Printed in U.S.A.

SIERRA CLUB, SIERRA CLUB BOOKS, and the Sierra Club design logos
are registered trademarks of the Sierra Club.

10 9 8 7 6 5 4 3 2

Dedicated to Toby Bellak
and the wise women of the Woodlands

INTRODUCTION

It is never too late to be what you might have been.
George Eliot

When we say "That's just my nature," we're saying much more than we realize. The behaviors that make up our *nature*—eating, sleeping, loving, mating, creating, talking, wandering, migrating, yearning, grieving, deceiving, dreaming—are as much a part of human biology as color, size, sex, and shape.

When we started our early years with instincts and intuitions that didn't exactly make sense (*or* they were criticized, *or* we were taught to overcome them), we learned to hide them, and then to bury them. Being told to get out of bed on time for school was so *hard* . . . eating when we weren't hungry didn't make *sense* . . . craving sex with the wrong person felt so *right.*

We are mute when it comes to naming accurately our own preferences, delights, gifts, talents. The voice of our original self is often muffled, overwhelmed, even strangled, by the voices of other people's expectations.
Julia Cameron

To survive in a world of conventions and confusions, we buried our quirks and irregularities (our authentic nature), bit by bit, to help us fit in. Can we still find it under all that rubble?

We don't always know what makes us happy.
We know, instead, what we think should.
Lucia Capacchione

Freud suggested that humans' daily struggle between our primitive/ authentic self (id) and our cultural/adopted self (superego) could lead to disaster. We've all had some disasters. Could they have been prevented? More important, can we prevent them in the future?

To see nature as *our nature* exposes a power within us—the power to become the person we want to be. This is a gift—available every day, wherever we are. We don't have to fly to exotic islands or climb giant mountains to find our true nature. It's in our city streets, vacant lots, backyards, streams, woods, puddles—it's in us.

You've got to find the force inside you.
Joseph Campbell

To find the nature of *my nature,* I use the wildlife around me as a Rorschach test—to see what part of the animal world I'm drawn to and which behaviors I identify with. I let my subconscious play an active role in this search. And, as in Rorschach tests, I see what I need to see.

Using nature to see myself isn't about wanting to *change* who I am—it's about uncovering my real nature—to *become* who I already am. Native Americans accept the idea that humans and animals share the same spiritual essence.

By studying and reading about the animals, birds, fish, insects, reptiles, etc., you encounter in your life, you can understand more about the circumstances

All living things have a common ancestry. Simple organisms gave rise to more complex ones. Variations gave rise to variations. Algae, worms, insects, reptiles, fish, and mammals evolved from single-celled beings. All these variations are part of my biology, and I can look at this mosaic of animal traits as part of my own evolution.

Does this imply that I'm programmed to *respond* to life, like a bird migrating in the spring or a locust emerging from its underground burrow? Or can I write the script of my own life, as I've always believed?

Since my *nature* includes millions of primitive instincts from which I can *choose* with consciousness—if I have a mind—I can decide which path to take. Knowing how to make good choices has become as natural as knowing the answers will come if I listen, knowing how to be a good animal.

Nature a Day at a Time describes common wildlife through the year. The pages weave Native American wisdom through a fabric of science and spirit, with threads of DNA showing the design of our evolutionary past. Eastern philosophy and intuition add the texture. Genes, schools, brain cells, and home life provide character. Use what's available. Just like the animals.

Anima: an' i ma \noun I a: SOUL, LIFE
b: an individual's true inner self

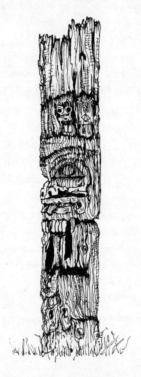

*A totem is any natural object, animal, or being to whose phenomena and energy
you feel closely associated with during your life. . . . Keep in mind that
each animal must be examined for its own characteristics and behaviors and
related specifically to your own individual life. Any correspondence
you can make is going to have some seeds of truth.*
Ted Andrews

NATURE

a Day at a Time

---

*"It's natural to die," he said again. "The fact that we make such a
big hullabaloo over it is all because we don't see ourselves as part of nature.
We think because we're human we're something above nature."*
Morrie Schwartz in *Tuesdays with Morrie,* by Mitch Albom

$\mathcal{A}$mber is fossilized resin, a thick gummy substance that drips
from trees. Resin protects trees from damage and works like a scab
to seal wounds. Resin also protects the trees from insect invasion
by trapping them as they walk or land on the thick, sticky goo.
When the liquid part evaporates, the resin turns hard, preserving
the trapped insect for thousands, sometimes millions, of years.

Amber is nature's Polaroid. To preserve one moment in time,
especially when that moment was millions of years ago, is one of
the most beautiful gifts from the past, no less significant than
the Last Supper.

Shown here is *Sphecomyrma freyi,* a wasp-ant
from New Jersey. This insect—with a head and
the stinger of a wasp, and a body and waist of
an ant—no longer exists.

*Thus, in nature life after death is a reality. The atoms of all matter have been
recycling—living, dying, being reborn—for millions of years.
Many a creature's atoms may be locked up for long periods in rocks, or
miles deep in the ocean, or high in the atmosphere.*
Valerie Harms in *The National Audubon Society Almanac of the Environment:
The Ecology of Everyday Life*

Spider fossils are relatively rare because spiders have no long-lasting bones or skeletons. We have few clues about their evolutionary past, but spiders sealed in **amber** provide a clear view of their existence millions of years ago.

The activity of ancient creatures captured in amber's avalanche shows the end of their life at the moment of contact with the sticky substance. *Dolomedes,* shown here, was a spider that lived more than a million years ago and was probably hunting or being hunted the moment before the tree's resin poured over it. The typically cautious spider evidently didn't avoid being overtaken by the path of the Superglue river.

Imagine that each insect, bird, snake, grain of sand, leaf, and pollen had an aura—which everything has—but imagine if we could *see it.* The distinction between the bird and the sky would be hazy and the separation between the ant and the tree would disappear—like the insect in amber. Imagine the whole universe in amber—all connected, all the same. When animals—including humans—walk, eat, sleep, and communicate, the auras blend, merge, grow, change, always overlapping and always connecting.

*Quantum theory has abolished the notion of fundamentally
separated objects. . . . It has come to see the universe as an interconnected
web of physical and mental relations whose parts are only
defined through their connections to the whole.*
Fritjof Capra in *The Tao of Physics*

January 3

*E*very living thing begins with a single cell,
a dot too small to see, containing all the
instructions to build a body with character—male/female, tall/short, shy/ag-
gressive, furry/scaled—with legs, nails,
brain, vision, voice, and virtue—all from
a speck.

The **river otter** (*Lutra canadensis*),
shown here, started from a cell similar to
that of the fish in its mouth—as did the
algae, bacteria, and crayfish in the river around
them.

What else do these cells have in store for us in
their infinite capacity?

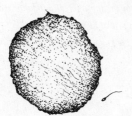

January 4

For billions of years, simple creatures like plankton, bacteria and algae ruled the earth. Then, suddenly, life got very complicated.
J. Madeleine Nash in "When Life Exploded"

$\mathcal{A}$ drop of water from any pond or puddle contains single-celled organisms like the **Euglena** shown here to the left. Neither plant nor animal, it is usually associated with **algae,** shown to the right, but *Euglena* has an eyespot and it wriggles in water by using its whip-tail. It eats, chases sunlight, reproduces, and grows; it has a nucleus and components that make it *alive.* Every other living cell shares these basic structures.

Looking at *Euglena* under a microscope, one is struck by its determination, as if it's on a mission, moving with a drive and purpose that only death will stop.

I am a member of a fragile species, still new to the earth, the youngest creatures of any scale, here only a few moments as evolutionary time is measured, a juvenile species, a child of a species. We are only tentatively set in place, error-prone, at risk of fumbling, in real danger at the moment of leaving behind only a thin layer of our fossils.
Lewis Thomas in *The Fragile Species*

It is never too late to be what you might have been.
George Eliot

$\mathcal{A}$moebas (*amoebae*), found in ponds, streams, puddles, and wet areas, are microscopic, one-celled creatures. Their name comes from the Greek *amoibē*, meaning "change." Shown here is an amoeba changing shape as it crawls along using its *pseudopods*, fake feet that serve to transport the jellylike creatures from one place to the next. They travel at speeds exceeding half an inch per hour.

Are they animals or plants? They are given their own kingdom, Protista, separate from the animal and plant kingdoms. Amoebas allow nature to tinker.

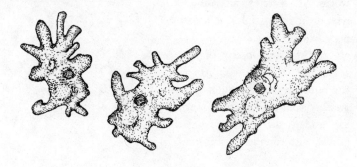

Nature serves as a good example of how trial and error can be used to make changes. Every now and then genetic mutations occur—errors in gene reproduction . . . occasionally a mutation provides the species with something beneficial and that change will be passed on to future generations. If there had never been any mutations from the first amoeba, where would we be now?
Roger von Oech in *A Whack on the Side of the Head*

---

*Take a gram of ordinary soil, a pinch held between two fingers, and place it in
the palm of your hand. You are holding a clump of quartz grains laced with
decaying organic matter and free nutrients, and about 10 billion bacteria.*
Edward O. Wilson in *The Diversity of Life*

*M*illions of bacteria, protozoa, fungi, algae, and nematodes live in
dirt. **Eel worms,** slippery microscopic creatures, are among these
soil citizens.

Shown here are various fungi with an
eel worm being ensnared by a **soil
fungus** (*Arthrobotrys anchonia*). Not
only does this fungus lasso the eel
worm, it secretes an adhesive,
making it impossible for the slippery worm to escape. The fungus digests the contents of its
prey, then moves on to continue
the hunt, weaving through threads of
another fungus, **Mucor** (shown here
as beaded threads) and **Circinella**
(stalks with rounded globes).

*Choose a cubic foot of earth, about anywhere that isn't paved; look closely
enough, and you'll find that thousands of different kinds of living things are
sharing that place, each one merrily surviving on something its neighbors couldn't
use for all the tea in China. I'm told that nine-tenths of human law is about
possession. But it seems to me we don't know the first thing about it.*
Barbara Kingsolver in *High Tide in Tucson: Essays from Now or Never*

---

*Observe always that everything is the result of change, and get used to
thinking that there is nothing Nature loves so well as to change
existing forms and to make new ones like them.*

Marcus Aurelius

*B*acteria, one-celled organisms, are found in fresh water, salt
water, air, dirt, skin, and intestines. They are shaped like globes,
rods, commas, bells, spirals, and sausages.

All of life's history includes bacteria, but for more than half
of this history, life was *only* bacteria. The first primordial cell with
a molecule of DNA to replicate
itself had a strategy to survive.
Fossils from 3.7 mil-
lion years ago show bacteria resembling *Streptococci*,
just a chain of cells programmed
for survival. *Streptococci* are the bacteria responsible for scarlet fever,
tonsillitis, and *strep* throat.

*We derive from a lineage of bacteria, and a very long line at that. Never
mind our embarrassed indignation when we were first told, last century, that
we came from a family of apes and had chimps as near cousins. That was
relatively easy to accommodate, having at least the distant look of a set
of relatives. But this new connection, already fixed by recent science beyond
any hope of disowning the parentage, is something else again. A first encounter,
the news must come as a kind of humiliation. Humble origins, indeed.*

Lewis Thomas in *The Fragile Species*

That "funny feeling" in our stomach after taking **antibiotics** comes from bacteria squirming in our intestines as they're being killed en masse.

After decades of using antibiotics, humans are losing their natural defenses to fight bacteria. The fittest bacteria are the ones to survive the onslaught from antibiotics, creating populations of superorganisms unaffected by the current antibiotics. In addition to that, new strains of bacteria are adapting so they actually thrive on antibiotics.

In the past, penicillin could kill bacteria from infections and colds, but a strain of bacteria developed, resistant to penicillin by producing an enzyme (*Penicillinase*) that breaks down the antibiotic before it can do its work.

Researchers continue to look for organisms in the earth to help fight diseases. Often, antibiotics in soil and mud are named for the place found; Miamycin was found in Miami, Nystatin in New York State, and Terramycin in Terre Haute.

All organisms that have ever lived—every animal and plant, all bacteria and all fungi—can look back at their ancestors and make the following proud claim: Not a single one of our ancestors died in infancy . . . they have what it takes to become ancestors—and that means to survive and reproduce.
Richard Dawkins in *River Out of Eden*

January 9

*V*iruses, like bacteria, are found in air, water, soil, dust, food, and skin. They can cause rabies, measles, yellow fever, flus, polio, mumps, and colds; their name means "poison."

What's the difference between bacteria and viruses? Similar to bacteria, viruses are in a hazy area between living and nonliving things, but are much smaller. Viruses can enter a cell and begin making copies of themselves—they actually exist *in* bacteria. They are, basically, a cluster of genes in a protective covering, unable to live independently. Bacteria, huge and sophisticated by comparison, provide a home for viruses to settle and multiply.

Shown here is the common bacteria **Staphylococcus,** which causes staph infections, next to much smaller viruses.

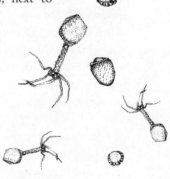

Viruses are coded program instructions written in DNA language, and they are for the good of the instructions themselves. The instructions say, "Copy Me and Spread Me Around" and the ones that are obeyed are the ones that we encounter. That is all. That is the nearest you will come to an answer to the question "What is the point of viruses?"
Richard Dawkins in *Climbing Mount Improbable*

*J*ust as a colony of ants surrounds an intruder, moving together as if directed, our bodies rally against foreign invasions with no more conscious effort on our part than breathing and digesting.

In our bodies, cells called **macrophages** come to our defense by battling with foreigners such as certain bacteria. Macrophages are considered the armored tanks of our immune systems. The one shown here, magnified hundreds of times, is "shooting" the bacteria **Escherichia coli** (*E. coli*), a simple and common inhabitant in our gut.

When an unfamiliar group of E. coli takes up residence inside us, perhaps from water in a foreign country, our intestines rebel at the invasion, reacting aggressively in a protective way. Diarrhea and exhaustion typically result from this internal battle.

The macrophage shown here uses sticky threads to lasso the sausage-shaped invaders. As prisoners, the bacteria are reeled into the body of the macrophage where enzymes dissolve the bacteria. The human host, in exchange for this service, provides shelter, breeding grounds, and nourishment for the parasites.

As a people, we have become obsessed with Health. There is something fundamentally unhealthy about all this. We do not seem to be seeking more exuberance in living as much as staving off failure, putting off dying. We have lost all confidence in the human body.

Lewis Thomas in *The Medusa and the Snail*

*M*ud is a bustling community of microscopic plants and animals. What makes sludge, mud, and manure smell so bad? Many bacteria that live in mammals and dirt produce methane gas and hydrogen sulfide, the smell of decay. The **methane bacteria** shown here, *Methanobacterium ruminantium,* magnified hundreds of times, live in cows' intestines.

These bacteria were probably one of the few life-forms that existed a few billion years ago. Most of our reserves of natural gas were produced by these and other bacteria of the past when Earth's early atmosphere contained no oxygen. Bacteria today commonly thrive in oxygen-deficient environments.

Today, nearly all life on Earth runs off energy harvested from the nearest star. Out there and down here are not separate compartments. Indeed, every atom that is down here was once out there.
Carl Sagan and Ann Druyan in *Shadows of Forgotten Ancestors*

Nematodes, commonly known as roundworms, are almost-microscopic white worms that thrash and coil energetically in soil. A spadeful of dirt has millions of them. They are the most wide-spread and varied of animals on Earth. All animals, including birds, rodents, snakes, insects, and humans, can be hosts for roundworms.

Roundworms burrow within the muscles, skin, glands, organs, intestines, eyeballs, liver, and nostrils, living off the fluids of their hosts. Some of these parasites are harmless, but some, like tapeworms, can grow to several yards and deprive the host of nourishment.

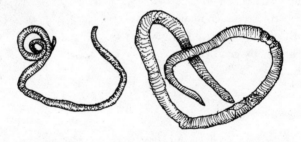

The nematodes shown here are roundworms (*Ascaris lumbricoides*) that live in human intestines. Males are slightly shorter and thinner than females and always have a coiled tail.

Parasites are part of the reason that we and most species have sex, rather than merely cloning ourselves in twain: we must stir our genes together in ever-changing combinations to develop resistance to parasites.
Natalie Angier in *The Beauty of the Beastly*

Tapeworms (*Cestoda*), like roundworms, commonly use human intestines as hosts. But unlike roundworms, they anchor themselves with suckers onto our flesh.

They enter our body when we eat pork, fish, or beef carrying the worms. After securing their position, the tapeworms begin to absorb all nearby nutrients from our intestines. New tapeworms are formed by "budding"—mating by transferring sperm to another segment, creating more and more segments while growing longer and more demanding of our food. Sooner or later the oldest ones leave the body, carrying eggs to an intermediate host—pig, cow, or fish.

The first rule is to keep an untroubled spirit. The second is to look things in the face and know them for what they are.
Marcus Aurelius

*T*he human body is a habitat for lice and **mites,** among many other microscopic animals. On our heads alone, are creatures so tiny they survive in eyelash follicles, around the pores by our noses, and in the crevices of our foreheads. If you scrape a little oil from your forehead and look at it under a microscope, you'll see many little creatures with spidery heads and legs squirming and biting with needle-sharp jaws.

Several species of mites are able to change into highly specialized forms when conditions become too dry or when food is scarce. They can hitchhike on insects or birds for a free ride to a more hospitable environment—then miraculously return to their original form.

> *The mite's digestive process yields so little waste that it doesn't even have*
> *an excretory opening. It need never get up to go to the bathroom.*
> *The follicle mite is, in truth, a couch potato's couch potato.*
> Richard Conniff in "Body Beasts," *National Geographic*, December 1998

$\mathcal{A}$ little larger than mites, head **lice** (*Pediculus capitis*) spend their entire life grazing and snacking on our scalps. We don't feel their bites when they first clamp down on our skin, but when their saliva mixes with our blood, we feel the prick. When we think we've scratched off the offending louse, it's probably still on our head, clinging to a hair shaft until it slides back down the shaft to the scalp prairie below. Their lobsterlike claws grip hair so tightly that even when hair is combed they slip through the comb's probing teeth.

Nits are the tiny eggs the female lays by attaching them to strands of hair. Each nit has its own tiny gas bubble in which to mature. After about five days, nymphs hatch and immediately begin feeding on scalp skin. Within a month females are mature enough to begin laying eggs.

But the beasts that live on our bodies are by no means all bad. A normal population of bacteria on the skin, for example, may actually benefit us by preventing infectious bacteria from gaining a beachhead. But if you tell people that a normal population can mean a hundred bacteria per square inch in the barren habitat of the shoulder blades (or millions in the sweltering armpit), they are liable to scrub themselves raw.

Richard Conniff in "Body Beasts," *National Geographic,* December 1998

*L*aboulbeniales are microscopic **fungi** (*Laboulbenia*) that grow exclusively *on* insects, without penetrating or damaging their host. The tiny fungus is only a bit bigger than a dust particle. One of 1,500 species of insect fungi, the one shown here is magnified by hundreds.

This fungus begins development as a two-celled spore and grows into an organism with male sex organs (the "legs") and a female sex organ (the large pear-shaped blob on the left).

Incredibly, each species grows on a specific part of its host's body—left wing cover of a beetle, back of a head, between the eyes, a certain leg, etc.

Inadequate though words are to portray what we see, imagine a weird science fiction garden of plants from another planet, but reduce them all to microscopic dimensions . . . no one of these would alter the bewilderment we feel in the presence of such a surfeit of forms so strange to us.
Harold J. Brodie in *Fungi: Delight of Curiosity*

*It is by looking at things for a long time that ripens you
and gives you a deeper understanding.*
Vincent van Gogh

Dung fungus (*Pilobolus*) begins its growth on cow and horse manure. The clear bulbs of the fungus shown here, explode and blast black caps from each bulb into the air, triggered by a mechanism controlled by temperature. As they drift down toward the ground, they land on plants, sticking on them with a gooey substance on each cap.

The caps are eaten by cows and horses grazing on grass, and once inside an animal's stomach, the caps dissolve, releasing spores. The spores eventually germinate in the animal's dung to begin another cycle.

Evolution, according to François Jacob, works "like a tinkerer who does not know exactly what he is going to produce but uses whatever he finds around him . . . to produce some kind of workable object."

*Perhaps it is not to be expected that many people would look
on a dung heap for an object of great beauty. . . .*
Harold J. Brodie in *Fungi: Delight of Curiosity*

The stuff of thought is not caged in the brain but is scattered all over the body.
Richard M. Bergland

Commonly found on old logs as yellow and orange shiny blobs, **slime molds** such as this one (*Dictyostelium discoideum*) get their energy from grazing on decaying material. These single-celled organisms act like stationary plants until they start eating. Then they become animal-like and slither to new locations. After changing into bulbous bodies-on-a-stalk, they become filled with spores. The spores, when released, germinate into little freestyle amoebas, crawling off to find bacteria to eat.

When their food supply runs out, the little creatures stream together, as if choreographed, gathering to form a pile of organized cells. This new slug-shaped blob moves forward like a single animal.

If animals and plants are the characters in nature's artwork, then slime molds must be the doodles and scribbles she made while figuring out what to paint next.

Look for ways to get mutations more quickly, new variety, different songs.
Fiddle around, if you must fiddle, but never with ways to keep
things the same, no matter who, not even yourself. Heaven,
somewhere ahead, has got to be a change.
Lewis Thomas in *The Medusa and the Snail*

January 19

. . . Predisposition is not predestination. Genes and neurotransmitters and hormones may tip the scales, but people are not robots programmed by genes. There is plenty of room for free will and conscience in how we behave and in how we judge the behavior of others.
Dean Hamer in *Living with Our Genes*

𝒯he **ant** shown here ate the spores of a fungus which began to grow *inside* the animal's body. The fungus can affect a particular area of the nervous system of its host, compelling it to climb high on the plant where the fungus needs to be for its own survival.

As the ant climbs, moving like a robot being commanded from within, the fungus absorbs the nutrients from the ant's system, eventually killing the ant—but not before it has reached a spot on the plant where the fungus can manufacture and drop spores onto lower leaves. When the next ant to come along eats the spores, the cycle begins again.

And if we do not know where consciousness itself emerges, how can we know where life in reality begins? Who knows, therefore, how far into the primordial past a "human" trait has its precursors?
Stuart Litvak and Wayne Senzee in *Toward a New Brain*

Earthstars (*Geastrum triplex*) are related to puffballs, woodland fungi made of round balls filled with spores. The "smoke" we see streaming from this common fungus is actually millions of spores.

Earthstars have two layers of skin surrounding their bubblelike structure, one of which splits as the fungus grows, creating a star-shaped base. When outside forces—rain or falling twigs—land on the soft earthstars, an explosion resonates inside the ball, releasing a mushroom-cloud of powdery spores into the air. Just a few raindrops can put enough pressure on an earthstar to create this volcanic eruption.

We have an irrational fungi-phobia that costs us billions of dollars, and it robs us of riches and valuable time. It leads us to damage our health by using huge amounts of synthetic fungicides and pesticides. Apparently we fear some fungi even more than the toxins that we use to kill them.
Bernd Heinrich in *The Trees in My Forest*

The true mystery of the world is the visible, not the invisible.
Oscar Wilde

*L*ichens are a combination of fungi and algae, each existing incognito while providing for the other's well-being. The body of a lichen is totally different from its independent members; together they form another entity, able to exist by offering what the other needs. Fungi absorb water and they "mine" minerals that algae need; algae create food, providing the sugars that fungi need.

Of the thousands of lichen species, all are tough and leathery, but that's where lichen likeness ends; they range in color, texture, size, and shape from leafy pale lichens growing on bark, shown right, to dark tubular ruffles growing in dirt, shown left.

New insights and theories quickly make many biology textbooks obsolete. One thing, however, will forever remain certain: As living things, we share an amazing number of characteristics with other forms of life. . . . It is only through looking at, and understanding the rest of the natural world that we can truly appreciate what it means to be "alive."
John Behler of the New York Zoological Society

*F*ruit flies (*Drosophila melanogaster*), tiny creatures no bigger than gnats, always seem to hover around fruit bowls. We casually swat them away, with no more consciousness than blinking our eyes. But what a role fruit flies have played in our knowledge of genetics.

Thomas Hunt Morgan was given the Nobel Prize in 1933 for his research on the fruit fly, in the now famous "fly room," where thousands of his subjects flew about freely.

The studies that Morgan conducted on the fruit fly were made possible because of his subject's short life cycle: fruit flies can produce a new generation every ten days or so from two hundred or more eggs. Larvae become adults in a few days and the adults are ready to mate within two days. They are attracted to the alcohol from rotting vegetation.

Drunken flies that carry a genetic mutation named "cheapdate" are helping scientists unravel one of life's mysteries: why some people can hold their liquor better than others. Ordinary fruit flies take 20 minutes to hit bottom. But the cheapdate mutants tumbled down in 15 minutes.

Associated Press, June 12, 1998

If we knew what makes a pine grow from a pine seed, and stay precisely
a pine through all the vicissitudes of its history, we should come
close to knowing what life really is.
Edmund W. Sinnott

As early as January, **pine pollen** starts drifting through the air, leaving a powdery yellow film on cars, windows, and any other smooth surface.

Although not as recognized as spring pollens, pine pollens, which are microscopic, winged balls, can be just as irritating to human noses.

Tiny Sputniks traveling through the lower sky, some pollen looks
like balls covered with spikes. Others are as football-shaped as the pupils of
alligators. Pine pollen is round, with what looks like a pair of ears attached to
each side. Their shapes make them move or fly at different speeds and
in different patterns, and there's little danger of the wrong
pollen swamping the wrong plant.
Diane Ackerman in *A Natural History of the Senses*

Nine-banded **armadillos** (*Dasypus novemcinctus*) are mostly found in the southeast United States, but they are steadily expanding their range northward. "Armadillo" comes from the Spanish word for "little armored thing." Their armor is a series of plates that protects them as they walk through prickly habitat. The nine bands are actually 2,500 overlapping plates.

Armadillos use their strong, sharp claws to dig burrows, where they stay during the day. At night they come out to dig for beetles, grubs, ant eggs, roots, and berries. They can eat two hundred pounds of insects a year, including fire ants.

While crossing roads to search for food or to extend their territory, armadillos are often startled by cars and jump *into* them, usually fatally.

Ted Andrews, in *Animal-Speak*, suggests moving dead animals from the road as a gesture of kindness . . . *so that other animals which scavenge upon it will not be hit by traffic as well. This is a tremendous honoring of the life of the animal and of nature. It says to the spirit of the animal, "Your life was beneficial."*

---

*It is clear there is a vocabulary of senses, a grammar beyond
that of a human making.*
Linda Hogan in "First People," from *Intimate Nature*

Armadillos always give birth to four identical babies of the same sex. This unusual birth is a result of one egg dividing after fertilization, eventually producing four embryos. Females can store sperm to be used for future fertilization. Embryo development can be delayed by two years after mating.

*Sex segregation during the breeding season is often facilitated by a
phenomenon known as sperm storage: most female animals have one or more
special organs or sites in their reproductive tract that allow them to store a cache
of sperm (from a prior mating) for a long time, using it to "inseminate"
themselves while foregoing heterosexual copulations.*
Bruce Bagemihl in *Biological Exuberance*

> *There are ways of knowing and being in the world that have not been*
> *available to our own human intelligence, that have only recently entered our*
> *perceptual maps, territories, and records. And together all the different*
> *intelligences equal a whole. This, I think, is the telling thing.*
> Linda Hogan in "First People," from *Intimate Nature*

$\mathcal{A}$ loud fly buzzing in the middle of winter is probably the awakening of a **housefly** (*Musca domestica*) who slipped through the door at the end of summer. A housefly can remain dormant until the first warmth reaches it, whether artificial or natural.

> *On the coldest day of winter I'll light a fire in the stove in this room. . . . Then*
> *a housefly the size of a Piper Cub will appear at the window inside. . . . In*
> *the way they gather at the windows to look out at the inhospitable winter,*
> *they remind me of elderly, well-stuffed gentlemen, members of a venerable and*
> *aristocratic club, who from the windows of the drawing room look out at*
> *the street, and seeing the changed world out there, are grateful to be old.*
> *I expect any minute one of these flies will abruptly rustle the*
> *pages of his* Times *and ring for a brandy.*
> Castle Freeman, Jr., in *Spring Snow*

God in His wisdom made the fly
And then forgot to tell us why
Ogden Nash

*M*uch larger and more robust than the common housefly, the **horsefly** (*Tabanus americanus*) is usually over an inch long.

Their eating habits are radically different between male and female, *and* between youth and adult: female horseflies suck blood from mammals, but males live on pollen and nectar, and their offspring feed on aquatic animals.

The female needs the protein in mammal blood to nourish her eggs. Her familiar erratic flight pattern is seemingly random as she buzzes wildly from flesh to plant, fields to streams—but each season she manages to lay thousands of eggs attached to vegetation near streams, ponds, and lakes. When the eggs hatch, the larvae fall into the water and spend the next two winters on the muddy bottom before emerging as adults. A raft of her eggs is shown here greatly enlarged.

Chaos theory shows us how apparently tiny and insignificant things can end up
playing a major role in the way things turn out. By paying attention to
the subtlety, we open ourselves to creative dimensions that
make our lives deeper and more harmonious.
John Briggs and F. David Peat in *Seven Life Lessons of Chaos*

Feathers of large meat-eating birds are used in making harpsichords—their quills pluck the strings, creating a resonance that no other bird feathers can produce.

Turkey vultures (*Cathartes aura*) are notorious meat eaters, particularly dead meat, which they can smell from miles away. They are opportunistic scavengers, but in the process, they clean up roadkill efficiently and relieve small wounded and sick animals from suffering.

They are protected from diseases that decaying animals carry by a sophisticated immune system. Their digestive tract contains chemicals that destroy bacteria that would be lethal to other animals; they let their excrement run down their legs to cleanse their feet from germs accumulated during feeding. As they eat, their heads probe deep into the carcasses of the dead animals, but, true to form, germs can't gather on their featherless heads.

Like all temperaments, the darkly emotional one has adaptive potential;
otherwise, it wouldn't be in such abundant supply.
Winifred Gallagher in *I.D.*

Whether or not we find what we are seeking
Is idle, biologically speaking.
Edna St. Vincent Millay

Eastern **cottontails** (*Sylvilagus floridanus*) are the most widely distributed rabbits in North America. They can produce several litters of many infants each year. "Breeding like a rabbit" is more than a cliché for these mammals, for the infants can begin breeding themselves just a few months after birth.

At night, cottontails emerge from hidden homes in thickets to feed on plants. The young follow the bright white tails of their parents through grasses. But the same white tail that guides the infants also signals predators of their presence. Rabbits are the most commonly preyed upon mammals; hawks, owls, foxes, dogs, humans, and coyotes all rely on the abundance of rabbits for food.

Winning and losing make sense to me only in terms of hunter and hunted, in
the natural order of things. Coyotes eat rabbits; rabbits never eat coyotes.
This may not be fair, but it is how it is.
Lynda Wheelwright Schmidt in *The Long Shore*

Great horned owls (*Bubo virginianus*) are one of the largest and most familiar of all North American owls. They are known as hoot owls because of their deep resonant *hoo hoo-hoo HOO HOO* that can be heard for miles.

The "horns" that give these owls their name are tufts, not ears, and are used in part for aggressive displays. The tufts are also used to funnel sound to the sensitive ears, which are farther down the sides of their heads—not as visible as the great horns.

The eyes of the great horned owls are so large they leave little room for muscles to move the eyes. Instead, the owl has fourteen vertebrae in the neck allowing the head to turn in the characteristic owl swivel. (Humans only have seven vertebrae in their necks.)

Owls use all their sharp senses—particularly hearing, but also vision and smell, and perhaps a sense that humans can't imagine—to hunt rats, rabbits, voles, snakes, gophers, and kittens. They are tolerant of humans, but if chicks are threatened, the parents won't hesitate to swoop down toward the intruder—as a warning—but further invasions might be met with more aggressive and more painful action.

This owl can rip the wings from a marsh hawk taken in midair as easily as some other owls remove moth wings.
Hamilton A. Tyler and Donald R. Phillips in *Owls by Day and Night*

January 31

*I*n January, the familiar call of the **great horned owl** reunites a mated pair, separated since the previous spring, to start their mid-winter courtship.

Great horned owls begin nesting as early as January. They take over the old nests of herons, hawks, crows, or abandoned baskets left by humans—anything large enough to hold the huge birds and all the bones and debris collected while feeding two owlets who eat their weight each day in mice and other small animals. Both male and female take turns incubating, and like most birds, develop an incubation patch where bare skin is supplied with extra blood.

By the time the nest becomes too crowded for the big babies and the trash, the owls begin to leave their nests in the spring, about the same time that other small birds and mammals are available as food.

While the majority of birds could be classified as "good housekeepers,"
some might, at best, be described as slobs. It isn't uncommon for the great
horned owl to accumulate so many dead animals in its nest that
its young succumb to disease.
Lester L. Short in *The Lives of Birds*

The **skunk**'s scientific name, *Mephitis,* means "a foul exhalation." This foul exhalation is an amber, oily liquid stored in musk glands beneath the tail. Two "nozzles" around the anus control the stream, like a garden hose, changing from a fine mist to a powerful stream of liquid beads. The odor molecules of this acrid, blinding fluid are powerful enough to be detected through glass, plastic, and metal.

A skunk typically uses restraint before using the odor defense system and will give warnings with a series of gestures including arching its back, shaking its head, raising its tail, and stamping its feet. When these warnings don't work, it assumes its firing position: upright on front legs and tail flared, it takes aim.

Using scent as a defense was adaptive for the skunk's survival. Body odor is a beneficial asset for humans, too, but, because we mask our odors with antiperspirants, we eliminate this defense. The scents we give off naturally could signal our interest to a potential mate, or perhaps give a warning to steer clear. Unfortunately, however, even if our odors were allowed to drift, we've lost our ability to "read" the signals the way animals can. In addition, the process of deodorizing clogs our lymph nodes with an accumulation of chemicals in sensitive areas, further weakening our natural capabilities.

Just trust yourself, then you will know how to live.
Johann Wolfgang von Goethe

People often change their sexual behavior during their lifetimes, making it impossible to state that a particular set of behaviors defines a person as gay....
from *Masters and Johnson on Sex and Human Loving*

Skunks are generally solitary, but females sometimes winter together in underground dens. In early spring, males and females get together to mate, but return to their solitary lifestyle after mating. Females give birth, usually in May, to four to eight blind, hairless kittens.

Many females seek a sexual relationship with a male in the spring—but sometime during the summer, they return to the company of females. Female pairing can be sexual or platonic, and many females remain solitary throughout the year.

Animals of the same sex build nests and homes together, and many homosexual pairs raise young without members of the opposite sex. Other animals regularly have partners of both sexes, and some even live in communal groups where sexual activity is common among all members male and female.... Amid this incredible variety of different patterns, one thing is certain: the animal kingdom is most definitely not just heterosexual.
Bruce Bagemihl in *Biological Exuberance*

*B*ecause they are programmed to become active at dusk, **skunks** are vulnerable to a few other night animals, also on the prowl for food. Most creatures steer clear of skunks, but the great horned owl, the skunk's main predator, attacks with no regard for the skunk's potent spray. Evidently, they are immune to the smell. (Similarly, some humans can't smell the skunk's offending odor, and some even claim they find it appealing.)

Do skunks ever spray each other? Yes, but usually accidentally when one is in the path of another one in the midst of defense.

Young skunks, at about six weeks, follow their mother, single file, into the woods to forage for food, taking the same route every night. They dig through dirt with their snouts, searching for insects. Little sneezes from skunks can be heard through the night as they clear their noses from dirt that gets clogged in their nostrils.

Mothers are protective of their kittens during the early weeks, and assume all the training and feeding responsibilities. Contact with the father ends after mating. Her relationship with a male doesn't begin again until the young are on their own.

If one way be better than another, that you may be sure is Nature's way.
Aristotle

*V*oles (*Microtus*) are some of the most familiar rodents in North America, but they are often mistaken for mice. They are, like mice, small and furry, but they have stockier bodies and smaller ears.

The range of behaviors among various species of voles is much more extreme than their rodent cousins. Mountain voles are loners that stay in isolated burrows until mating season, when they become wild and promiscuous. By contrast, prairie voles live sociably in communities, displaying affection and constantly communicating with one another. The gentler prairie voles mate for life, while the mountain voles will seek any and all mates, without continuing the relationship after mating.

Neurophysiological researchers found a chemical responsible for the difference in behaviors between species. 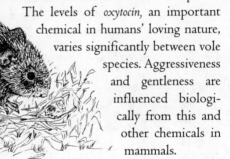 The levels of *oxytocin*, an important chemical in humans' loving nature, varies significantly between vole species. Aggressiveness and gentleness are influenced biologically from this and other chemicals in mammals.

Such a study makes one wonder about the complex role that oxytocin plays in human relationships. Are oxytocin levels lower in people characterized as "loners," in abusing parents, in children suffering from the solitary nightmare of autism?

Diane Ackerman in *A Natural History of Love*

. . . The power of each hormone turns out to extend far beyond physiology.
Nature is, after all, a tight fisted engineer, likely to use the
same materials to perform many tasks at once. . . .
Natalie Angier in *The Beauty of the Beastly*

*V*oles spray their paws with urine and leave trails
of suggestive pheromones as they walk, signaling *this is my territory*. A male prairie vole
will show aggressive behavior when another male intrudes, threatening to take
his mate or territory.

Pheromones not only mark territory,
but can trigger ovulation and
courtship behavior. *Pheromone* comes from
the Greek *pherein*, meaning "to
carry" and *hormon*, meaning
"to excite."

. . . Immediately after a male has
mated with a female, he shows signs of
preferring her to other females, not only
by cuddling with her, grooming her
fur, and exhibiting other familiar marks of affection, but also by attacking
strange voles of either sex that approach his turf. Aggression is one way of
expressing attachment, and a post
coital prairie vole is a pugnacious fellow to behold.
Natalie Angier in *The Beauty of the Beastly*

February 6

---

*. . . Because it often resembles the trunk next to it, [bark] captures our
imagination about as much as the nearby telephone pole.*
Kjell B. Sandved in *Bark*, by Ghillean Tolmie Prance and Anne E. Prance

Bark is the disposable layer of a tree that most of
us don't think twice about. But bark supports a
community of wildlife by providing food, hiding
places, mating areas, and nest-building material.
Insects, birds, mammals, reptiles, and humans
make use of this lumpy, taken-for-granted, afterthought of a tree. It may be the most overlooked and underrated part of our trees.

*Objects are concealed from our view not so much
because they are out of the course of our visual
ray . . . as because there is no intention of the eye
toward them. We do not realize how far and widely,
or how near and narrowly, we are to look.*
Henry David Thoreau

$\mathcal{P}$ine sawflies (*Neodiprion pinetum*) are actually wasps (they have two pairs of wings), but they don't sting. The female uses a "saw" at the end of her abdomen to cut through a pine needle in which she lays one hundred eggs or more. The eggs mature inside the pine needles, with unfertilized eggs producing only males. A pine needle with a series of neat and tiny brown slashes is usually the work of a female sawfly.

From the eggs, larvae emerge with the look and behavior of butterfly caterpillars, but entomologists are careful not to call them caterpillars, because they are indeed part of the family of wasps, bees, and ants. The caterpillarlike larva is shown below an egg-filled pine needle.

The one-inch larvae eventually spin themselves into cocoons in which they pupate, emerging in the spring as mature sawflies. As adults, they continue to live as solitary animals, usually only socializing to find a mate, after which they return to their solo lifestyle.

. . . Aloneness is a biological and psychological essential and just as important as the heavily documented need for attachment. By my definition it includes the need to retreat psychologically (and at times, physically) in order to modify stimulation and to constitute or reconstitute how one functions—by oneself.
Ester Schaler Buchholz in *The Call of Solitude*

Some people may crave many hours by themselves; others may find
sufficient solace in small doses of separate time. Regardless of the dosage, solitude
is a deep, soothing, and persistent call in life. . . . alonetime is vital to
our peace and existence, a route open to us for survival.
Ester Schaler Buchholz in *The Call of Solitude*

Sociability among insects ranges from ants, which live in colonies of millions, to antlions, which spend almost their entire life by themselves underground. Among bees the range of social interaction varies from dense hive populations to bees living alone in burrows.

Variations of aloneness span the animal world. But humans are the only species who apologize, defend, justify, hide, judge—or worse, ignore—their need for solitude.

Female **solitary bees,** such as the mining bee (*Andrena*) shown here, dig long underground tunnels in which they lay an egg in a single cell. They spend the winter alone, separated by cells, until the spring, when they gather nectar and begin the process of finding mates. After mating, the solitary bees return to life alone.

And yet, verbal and facial expression are still an effort for me.
Only when alone, or with an animal, do I relax.
Lynda Wheelwright Schmidt in *The Long Shore*

Prairie dogs (*Cynomys*) were named for their doglike bark. They are members of the squirrel family and live in lonely, dry, brushy areas.

In their isolated prairies, these rodents are extremely sociable, with complex traditions and behaviors. They show signs of affection by grooming, touching faces, tumbling, and fondling family members and neighbors.

The chemicals exchanged from "kissing" are a way to transfer information between prairie dogs.

I wasn't kissing her,
I was just whispering in her mouth.
Chico Marx
in *Marx Brothers Scrapbook*
by Groucho Marx and Richard J. Anobile

A **prairie dog** colony offers protection from dozens of stalking predators. Their complex language of thumps, barks, and body gestures relays information about specific events nearby: "approaching hawk," "big human hunting," "coyote to the west."

Their social system is regimented by structure and rules such as the movement of the very old and the very young to the fringes of a colony.

Prairie dogs learn and practice skills such as diving quickly into their tunnel openings to prepare for inevitable threats to their safety. Despite the time spent guarding their communities, prairie dogs spend hours at play each day.

No other animal, except for perhaps the wolf, epitomizes the idea of community more than the prairie dog. A prairie dog community is always filled with activity.
Ted Andrews in *Animal-Speak*

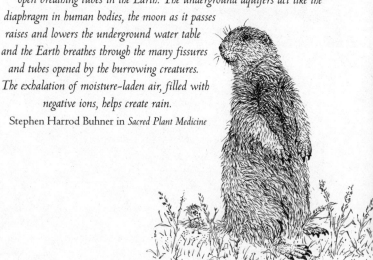

Prairie dogs construct complex systems of burrows that can extend for ninety feet with several side streets on either side of the main tunnel. The creative construction allows for a circulation system where stale air is sucked from the tunnel at one end as the lower entrance draws in fresh air.

The benefits to the prairie land are inestimable. Not only do the tunnels aerate the soil, their constant mowing increases protein content of the soil, earning them the title of fertilizing machines.

There is an old Navajo warning that if you kill off the prairie dogs there will be no one to cry for rain. . . . In fact, the burrowing animals, like prairie dogs, open breathing tubes in the Earth. The underground aquifers act like the diaphragm in human bodies, the moon as it passes raises and lowers the underground water table and the Earth breathes through the many fissures and tubes opened by the burrowing creatures. The exhalation of moisture-laden air, filled with negative ions, helps create rain.

Stephen Harrod Buhner in *Sacred Plant Medicine*

Water bears, or tardigrades, look like tiny, eight-legged bears. They are microscopic creatures living in gutters, ditches, ponds, mosses, lichens, soil, and plant litter. Straining a cup of water after a rain will expose at least a few of them.

Their scientific name, *Tardigrada,* means "slow mover." To walk, water bears lift three stubby legs on one side as the legs on the other side stay down—all this seems to happen in slow motion.

They can survive for fifty years or more, even in temperatures as low as –400 degrees Fahrenheit. If their ditch or gutter dries up, they live in a state of hibernation called *cryptobiosis,* which means "hidden life." When they are in this dormant state, water bears are as light as dust particles—a breeze will pick them up and carry them to another area. As soon as they contact water, they become active and begin their slow walk toward food.

Organisms fashion all these bio-minerals with great precision and under conditions that would make many processing engineers envious. Over and over they demonstrate that whatever engineers can do, nature can do better and on a much finer scale.

Elizabeth Pennisi in "Natureworks" in *Science News*

*O*ak leaves contain tannic acid, which discourages bacteria. The leaves are then slow to disintegrate when they fall. Eventually the tannic acid becomes part of the soil, ultimately helping future oak seeds to sprout.

Just like the seed of an idea, some acorns sprout, some don't. But none will grow if they're pulled up just to check on their progress.

The same life force that grows an oak from an acorn, a mountain from the earth's molten core, a stream from the spring's thaw, a child from an egg and sperm, an idea from the mind of a human being is present in all things, all thoughts and all experiences. There is no place where God is not.
Joan Borysenko in *Pocketful of Miracles*

*Carefully observe what way your heart draws you, and then
choose that way with all your strength.*
Hasidic saying

The common name **bachelor's buttons** (*Centaurea cyanus*) may have come from an old custom when men put flowers in their buttonholes while courting a sweetheart; if the flower stayed fresh, it was a good sign the romance would continue, but if the flower wilted, his beloved didn't love him.

Another old story claims that women once wore bachelor's buttons to signal their ability to marry.

*Men have often presented women with flowers, chocolates, perfumes,
and other pleasurable treats to put them in a romantic mood.
"Awaken her senses first" seems to be the unstated motto of suitors. In any case,
flowers are the plants' sex organs, and they evoke the sex-drenched,
bud-breaking free-for-all of spring and summer.*
Diane Ackerman in *A Natural History of Love*

---

*T*he **tufted titmouse** (*Parus bicolor*), a sociable and energetic little songster, has easily adapted to urban settings, including city parks, roadside fields, and backyards.

Titmice hang out with flocks of chickadees, nuthatches, kinglets, and other small migratory songbirds. Staying with their own and other flocks gives the titmouse protection—safety in numbers—and allows more free time for feeding and resting. Birds feed with their heads down, a vulnerable position, but when hundreds of pairs of eyes are scanning nearby bushes and trees for hidden danger, a signal of danger is more likely and can mean life or death.

The safety of a flock provides defense against a predator—flock mates can rally together against a large hawk, where a single bird would lose its chance to live if confronted. When a flock senses danger, a group may respond by tightening up their numbers—a common animal strategy. As the group forms a tight unit, perhaps several birds at the fringes will flutter and create enough chaos to confuse a stalker who initially focused on one single straggler.

Nothing was more dangerous than being an outcast, losing the safety and nourishment of the group. We still fear that isolation worse than anything. For much or our evolution, being an outsider was fatal. Small wonder loneliness frightens us as it does.
Diane Ackerman in *A Slender Thread*

$\mathcal{A}$ common shrub in damp habitats, **pussy willows** (*Salix*) are one of the first signs of spring. Their buds are called *catkins,* meaning "small cats," because of their soft, kitten-like fur. Each catkin is actually a bunch of flowers.

Bud scales protect each catkin from the cold. As the days grow warmer and the catkins larger, the buds fall off. By the time the catkins are about an inch, tiny flowers emerge, often seen in February.

A tiny green leaf or shoot appearing magically on a cutting put in water or in the earth is like a revelation, almost an epiphany—the appearance of the Other—a life with its own laws.
Jane Hollister Wheelwright in *The Long Shore*

Pussy willows grow two kinds of flowers; male and female—flowers on a pussy willow stalk are either all male or all female, never mixed.

Pussy willow pollen, from the male, is yellow and light. It's easily carried by either air or insects. When pollen reaches a female plant, seed production begins. In males, leaves push their way out of the buds, creating a little collar around the stem.

. . . While we readily accept that a healthy seed can't grow into a plant without the right soil, light, and water, and that a feral dog won't behave like a pet, we resist recognizing the importance of environment in our own lives.

Winifred Gallagher in *The Power of Place*

*And the day came when the risk to remain tight in a bud was more
painful than the risk it took to blossom.*

Anaïs Nin

𝓕emale **pussy willows,** without the yellow pollen that male flowers produce, are less colorful than the males. Their capsules
continue to grow; eventually silky fluff
balls containing seeds pop out, fly into
the air, and float until they land in a
wet, shady area. The seed can sprout
within twelve to twenty-four hours.
Within a few days, a plant emerges.
In less than four months, the plant
is about a yard tall—more than a
thousand times its seed size.

*The indescribable innocence and beneficence
of Nature—of sun and wind and rain, of
summer and winter—such health, such cheer,
they afford forever!... Shall I not have
intelligence with the earth? Am I not partly
leaves and vegetable mould myself?*

Henry David Thoreau

White-breasted nuthatches (*Sitta carolinensis*) are often seen clinging to trees upside down as they hunt for ants, caterpillars, beetles, and weevils hidden in bark and crevices. Their long, sharp claws anchor securely into the bark as they move *down* the trees, inspecting the bark below. The nuthatches also wedge nuts and seeds into the trees, and hack at them until they crack.

During the winter, white-breasted nuthatches gather with woodpeckers, chickadees, titmice, and a few other small birds to form loose flocks of foraging birds. The nuthatches act as sentries to call out warnings to their flock mates, letting them know a hawk or other predator is in the area. The birds heed the warnings and take off for safer areas. However, the seemingly altruistic nuthatch uses the same warning calls to chase other small birds away from a good feeding spot so it can move in and eat without competition.

Animal communication just isn't that complicated. Nor is it that simple.
It is always a matter of urgency. It is of the moment, of the entire situation that
confronts an animal, and thus, always "important." Animals in nature
do not engage in small talk, or in any form of talk at all.
Eugene S. Morton and Jake Page in *Animal Talk*

*C*ommon shrews (*Sorex cinerus*) are the world's smallest mammals and their range of habitats exceeds any other North American mammal. They can live in grasslands, wetlands, forests, hills, farms, and fields. Not only do they live anywhere, they eat almost anything, hunt anytime, and attack anything they can, even animals twice their size.

Nests are built from careless arrangements of leaves and grasses. Four to ten babies, the size of honeybees, are born between spring and fall. Shortly after birth, the tiny animals start hunting aggressively, challenging animals much larger than themselves.

These fearless bundles of energy stay mostly out of sight, but not from fear of predators; most meat eaters avoid shrews because of a strong unpleasant musk they release from a stomach gland when threatened.

We live with the fact that some of our desires, fears, and motives are beyond the ability of our rational self-reflective consciousness to explain.

Laurence Miller in *Inner Natures*

"*H*ot and smoky, almost irreverent. Imagine W. C. Fields extinguishing a cigar on your tongue," describes the sting of a yellow jacket according to Justine O. Schmidt, an entomologist with the U.S. Department of Agriculture.

Yellow jackets (*Vespula*) are more aggressive than most bees and wasps; they pierce skin with their stingers and inject a hot, burning fluid. Biochemists praise the venom as an ingenious and elegant blend of molecules with an uncanny ability to spread through the body within minutes. The chemicals can cause shock, respiratory difficulties, mood swings, confusion, weakness, headaches, nausea, and unconsciousness—all from one drop of liquid.

Females spend the winter under leaves and soil in a dormant state. During this time, small mammals may dig up the nests to eat the quiet wasps inside. If they survive the winter, the yellow jackets begin building nests. During this nest-building and egg-laying period, they are the most aggressive.

It's easy to imagine how discovering the biological "cause" of aggression could lead to it being declared "normal" and therefore acceptable. If someone is naturally aggressive, then they should be free to act out their genetic destiny. . . . Why shouldn't a man be able to get in touch with his inner gangster?
Dean Hamer in *Living with Our Genes*

A visitor once asked George Bernard Shaw why he kept no cut flowers in his home, since he was so fond of them. "So I am," he said. "I'm very fond of children, too, but I don't cut off their heads and stick them in pots all over the house."

Rose hips are the fruit of a pollinated rose. They contain ten to one hundred times as much vitamin C as other fruits or vegetables.

Rose hips contain the ovaries of the rose, and they can be seen at the base of the bud, developing before the rose blooms.

When the rose opens, insects are attracted to the scent. The ovaries are fertilized and the rose hip swells. After fertilization the flower is no longer needed to attract pollinators, and it dies, leaving the swollen rose hip to develop seeds.

This is the true joy in life, the being used for a purpose recognized by yourself as a mighty one, the being thoroughly worn out before you are thrown into the scrap heap; the being a force of Nature instead of a feverish selfish little clod of ailments and grievances, complaining that the world will not devote itself to making you happy.
George Bernard Shaw

Peregrine falcons (*Falco peregrinus*) are the fastest birds in the world, racing through the sky at speeds approaching two hundred miles an hour. Their spectacular aerial displays include diving toward Earth from heights of up to a mile while somersaulting and barrel-rolling in dramatic performances not seen in any other bird. And if these aerial stunts aren't enough to take their own breath away, they can also attack and snatch small birds from the sky that they pass to their mates—all in midair.

The speed is defiant. Sheer gravity cannot match it; nor can any device in the natural world. Certainly the otherwise fleet pigeon cannot; before it can feint or dash away the peregrine hits it feetfirst with a colossal wallop, breaking its back and spraying its feathers in a puff like a down pillow burst in a kids' bedroom fight.
Bruce Brooks in *On the Wing*

Bird's nest fungi (*Cyathus olla*), related to puffballs, are pea-sized cups commonly found around gardens, compost piles, and old, damp boards. These fungi are easily overlooked because of their size and color, blending in well with their surroundings.

Miniature baskets hold several spore-filled "eggs," each of which is held inside by a cord. How are the spores released from their tethered position inside their cup? Raindrops, as powerful as a blast from a fire hose to a tiny fungus, splash inside the cup, forcing the eggs out. Each egg flies out with a cord dangling from behind, soaring through the air like a gaucho's bola. It wraps around the first plant in its path, entangling itself to its new host.

Ultimately, the spores are distributed when an animal eats the host plant. Inside the animal's digestive tract, the case is dissolved, releasing spores that are ready to germinate when they travel out with the dung.

One cannot escape a feeling of profound respect . . . and one is delighted by the beauty inherent not so much in the form or colour of Bird's Nest Fungi as in the means whereby they are able to compete successfully with other living things in the great contest for continuing survival.
Harold J. Brodie in *Fungi: Delight of Curiosity*

*E*very once in a while, a patch of dirt seems to appear on new snow with no explanation. And strangely enough, when you walk over to investigate, the dirty patch disappears. What is this? Millions of **snow fleas** (*Achorutes nivicolus*) emerge from under the snow on sunny winter days to mate. Huge swarms appear like pepper flakes sprinkled on the white of newly fallen snow.

Snow fleas are a species of springtails, tiny inconsequential creatures that live in leaf litter. Their magical appearance and disappearance comes from their ability to "spring" with a high-energy blast using their *furculum,* an organ with a trigger mechanism. This organ is held tight against the underpart of their body by a latch. When the latch is released, the springtail catapults several inches. This blast is faster than our eyes can process, so one blink is enough time for them to disappear.

Nature tries to show us every day that all forms of life can teach us. As we learn to listen to Nature, we break down our outworn perceptions. We find that magical creation is the force of life inherent in all things. And it is this, above all else, that Nature teaches to those who will learn from Her.
Ted Andrews in *Animal-Speak*

Huge flocks of **common grackles** (*Quiscalus quiscula*) gather in the winter in parks, fields, and on lawns. Bright yellow eyes and iridescent bodies distinguish grackles from their crow neighbors.

Grackles have sleek black feathers with bronze and purplish hues. To keep the feathers shiny and healthy, grackles, like most other birds, spend time each day preening. By running their feathers through their beak, oils secreted from a special gland above the tail are spread through the feathers. Preening also removes fungi, lice, and bacteria from the feathers.

Grackles also use a method called "anting" to soothe skin irritated by parasites such as feather lice, who feed on blood at the base of the feathers. Anting makes use of the antibiotic substance in an ant's body— the birds either squeeze the ants or let them "graze" through the feathers. But grackles also use flowers as an anting tool. Marigolds contain a chemical, *pyrethrum,* to control the parasites irritating their skin. They rub the flowers through their feathers, sending the powerful chemical to the areas where mites and other irritants exist.

Admittedly in some situations, again usually those created by people, birds act in ways that appear stupid. But such actions can often be attributed to behavior that is adaptive in natural circumstances. Occasional stupidity, moreover, does not negate intelligence either in birds or in humans.

Alexander F. Skutch in *The Minds of Birds*

Common ravens (*Corvus corax*) are similar to common crows but much larger, with heavier bills, and, compared with the sociable crows, ravens tend to be loners. However, ravens gather with other ravens when it benefits their survival.

A dead animal, which is a bonanza for scavenging ravens, will be thoroughly checked out from a distance before indulging. The bravest ravens will be the ones to approach, to learn if the animal is indeed dead, or if other scavengers are guarding from a distance. Less brave ravens watch from the side-lines, waiting until they see that the coast is clear before joining in. The risk-taking ravens yell and scream over a dead carcass, letting the neighborhood know how courageous they are, and more important, that food is now available and safe.

. . . Some seem to positively court *danger. For example, ravens have been seen diving at a resting wolf, or sneaking up from behind to peck at its tail, only to jump away at the last moment to escape its snapping jaws. . . . Male birds may alternate between acts of bravery and courtship of female onlookers. They sometimes even treat risk-taking as a privilege. . . .*

Frans de Waal in *Good Natured*

There is no love sincerer than the love of food.
George Bernard Shaw

The scientific name for the **fish crow,** *Corvus ossifragus,* means "bone-breaking raven," an apt term for these relatives of the raven—their strong beaks can crunch the hard bones of small fish—their main food and the reason for their common name. Like ravens, they are scavengers, but live mainly along coastal areas.

Because they live by waterways, fish crows take advantage of nearby shorebird rookeries to steal the eggs and chicks from their nests. Removing the contents of a nest and munching down a few big eggs or tiny heron chicks is as natural for a fish crow as it is for a human to tear into a bucket of crispy fried chicken—and the action satisfies some primal need not only to attack food, but to *feel* and *hear* the explosion of crunching through a hard outer covering to the soft flesh inside.

Be a good animal, true to your animal instincts.
D. H. Lawrence in *The White Peacock*

*C*ommon crows (*Corvus brachyrhynchos*) live in every state and every habitat—roadsides, backyards, parks, farms, and woods. They gather in roosts of hundreds of thousands every day, calling with a magnitude and urgency that is hard to ignore.

Crows have a complex language of *caws*, with about two dozen different vocalizations including screams, cackles, rattles, and sharp notes— each translated by other crows as warnings, food alerts, love messages, and general reporting. Small talk? Birds don't waste their breath just to be heard. An economy of sounds provides just the necessary information to be heard above the busy traffic noise of other roosting birds.

Crows aggressively attack and pursue birds that are much larger than themselves. Aggressive temperaments respond to stress by boldly attacking, while shy temperaments respond by carefully considering options. The bold are impulsive; the shy, thoughtful.

Neither e = mc² nor Paradise Lost *was dashed off by a party animal. . . . The ranks of Nobel and Pulitzer prizewinners may be filled with sensitive souls who think beautiful thoughts, but from day to day the bold have more fun. Stress that strains or even breaks high-strung spirits merely stimulates theirs.*

Winifred Gallagher in *I.D.*

Regulars in New York City's Central Park witnessed the start of a love story in the early 1990s, as Pale Male, a young **red-tailed hawk** (*Buteo jamaicensis*), courted an older female. They mated, produced a nest, and took turns sitting on the eggs. However, Central Park crows harassed the hawks with a determination that eventually injured both, almost fatally. The female, with a broken wing, was taken to the Raptor Trust in New Jersey. Pale Male was treated for a concussion and released four days later back in Central Park.

Marie Winn, in *Red-Tails in Love*, describes the events that followed Pale Male's recovery, finding another love (named Chocolate) in January, and discovering First Love again after a long separation.

They made an odd couple, a mature female who had hooked up with a young and inexperienced male. His lack of savoir-faire was evident: on March 23rd, as the female was perched on a stanchion in front of the Delacorte Theater below Belvedere Castle, the light-colored red-tail was observed as he landed on top of her and tried to consummate their union.

But he was doing it at the wrong end.

Marie Winn in *Red-Tails in Love*

He was still a browntail that spring, too young for love. Nevertheless and notwithstanding, when the female (this one with a bright red tail) showed up at the beginning of March, Pale Male courted and won her.
Marie Winn in *Red-Tails in Love*

The familiar high-pitched screams of **red-tailed hawks** are easily heard as they circle high in the sky during the day. Their sharp eyesight can detect the least movement in grass far below.

Red-tails begin courting in the spring, usually after they are fully mature, which might not occur until after their first or second year. Often during their first years of development, they migrate to areas they will never visit again, perhaps passing by future mates. By the time they are mature, they have developed the distinctive rust-colored tail that gives them their name.

Hawk sex, like nest-building, is triggered by hormones stimulated by the length of daylight. . . . The sex act itself is not particularly dramatic. The male comes in for a landing from above, his talons extended in a posture the texts call the "talon drop." He lands on her back, keeping his balance by slight wing movements. The actual hawk sex act rarely lasts for more than five seconds, at least not as performed by the Fifth Avenue hawks and carefully timed by the hawkwatchers.
Marie Winn in *Red-Tails in Love*

$\mathcal{D}$efense instincts show up early in **red-tailed hawks.** A red-tailed chick, long before it can fly, will display a protective gesture for a sibling when threatened. The protectiveness continues as they mature; parents, to protect the chicks, have been seen transporting the helpless birds to safety by carrying them in their claws.

Nests of red-tailed hawks are large affairs mainly built with sticks and lined with almost any available soft material such as grass.

. . . Knowing that the increasing length of days in the spring stimulates the birds' pituitary gland to release certain chemicals and knowing that one of these triggers the gathering of twigs, and then when the nest reaches a certain stage of completion, another chemical kicks in—leading the birds to gather different *materials for the lining—this knowledge caused many of us to reconsider our own behavior: might far more of it be triggered by instinctive messages we cannot understand or control?*

Marie Winn in *Red-Tails in Love*

***

*C*opperheads (*Agkistrodon*) are often confused with young cotton-mouths because of the similar markings. Both are pit vipers and highly dangerous, but cottonmouths are always by water, while copperheads are often found far from water in dry, wooded areas or in wide-open prairies.

Copperhead populations grow slowly over years; for every ovulating female, hundreds of males are available, so most viper females can be choosy. Besides, they only mate once every three to five years, adding to the lopsided supply and demand. Males fight intensely, sometimes for days, to mate with one of the few available females.

. . . Woe to the snake that cannot stand its ground.
Among copperheads, a trounced male ends up so demoralized that for days
afterward even far punier males, which normally would be loath
to pick a fight, will take on the loser and defeat it.
Natalie Angier in *The Beauty of the Beastly*

*E*astern moles (*Scalopus aquaticus*) eat insect larvae and worms underground, rather than grass and plants as their reputation suggests. Because of their high metabolism, they eat constantly, moving across lawns and fields, aerating the soil as they go. Their huge, powerful feet and pointy snout help excavate their long complex tunnels.

Beetles and other burrowing insects fall into mole tunnels as the insects swim through the dirt, providing easy meals for the moles.

Moles socialize only once a year, in the spring, and only to mate. Several weeks after mating, the female gives birth to about four babies who mature within weeks to begin their solitary lives. Males and females maintain separate lives, even when caring for the young who are raised solely by females.

An ironic footnote is that, as men become the New-Age sensitive guys women want, some women are less able to find them sexually attractive because they strike too many feminine chords. I find this amusing because it reminds me that we're dealing with ancient hungers, ancient drives, and trying to adapt them to a society for which they weren't designed.

Diane Ackerman in *A Natural History of Love*

Bombardier beetles (*Brachinus*) mature inside the empty remains of other insects. The larvae of these beetles become parasites on pupating insects, eating them, then using their outer shell to bed down for the winter.

In the spring they emerge as mature bombardier beetles, ready to begin their search for food and sex.

As defense, the bombardier beetle sprays a powerful toxic liquid from special glands. Chemical reactions just before firing heat the liquid to the temperature of boiling water—and the pressure forces a stream of fluid from its abdomen with a loud *pop*.

The bombardier beetle can shoot in different directions, taking aim accurately, and reload, all within a second or less. The brown-staining liquid can be fired twenty to thirty times.

A master of defense and weaponry, the bombardier can swivel its gun turret,
aim straight at an intruder, and fire a twenty-six-mile-per-hour blast
of searing irritants, not in a continuous stream, but as a salvo of
minute explosions. This "pulsed jet" is oddly similar to the propulsion
system used in the German V-1 buzz bombs of World War II.
Diane Ackerman in *The Rarest of the Rare*

. . . In an environment filled with predators or their modern equivalents, having some fussbudgets and worriers around is adaptive for the group. That's why they stay so well represented in the gene pool.
Winifred Gallagher in I.D.

Race runners (*Cnemidophorus*) are long-tailed lizards that race nervously from spot to spot, constantly turning their heads frantically, as if needing to check to see who's chasing them. Their nickname, "whip-tail," comes from their long tail swishing erratically from side to side as they prowl.

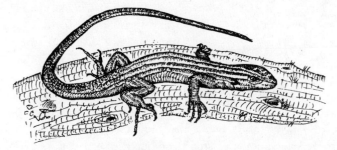

According to *Peterson's Field Guide to Reptiles and Amphibians*, several species of race runners are unisexual or bisexual; those who produce young do so by developing unfertilized eggs. "Males are completely unknown in some of these species . . . there is some evidence to indicate that such males may be hybrids between the unisexual form and a bisexual species inhabiting the same area."

The time has come, I think, when we must recognize bisexuality as a normal form of human behavior.
Margaret Mead in *Redbook* magazine, 1975

*C*entipedes (*Scutigera coleoptrata*), despite their name, don't have one hundred legs. Instead, they have between 15 and 173 pairs of legs, depending on the species. Separate from both insects and spiders, they are in a class of creatures of their own, *Chilopoda*.

Their first pair of legs serve as modified fangs, with poisonous claws that can inflict painful, but not too serious, bites on humans. They move rapidly through houses, or over logs and leaves, hunting for cockroaches, beetles, scorpions, and earthworms.

Centipedes reproduce without actually mating. A male leaves a package of sperm for the female to pick up, which she does, but stores it for later fertilization.

After the eggs are fertilized, the young centipedes emerge with only seven body segments, but, as they molt, they add more until fully grown, sometimes with almost two hundred segments.

Any living cell carries with it the experience of a billion years of experimentation by its ancestors.
Max Delbrück

Although similar to centipedes, **millipedes** (*Narceus americanus*) generally have much different life habits. Instead of hunting for insects, millipedes slowly graze over moist leafy areas, eating decaying plant matter. For protection, their bodies have a hard shell, which can curl into a tight ball when threatened.

Lacking the centipede's sting, millipedes have another defense system: a built-in arsenal of hydrogen cyanide, a deadly gas, which can be fired from cannonlike holes along their sides. The holes are connected to a two-chambered gland, each storing the necessary ingredients to make ammunition. This arsenal is fired either from specific ports or all at once depending on the attacker's position. Not all millipedes have this potent arsenal, but all release a strong, unpleasant odor when threatened.

The root of these responses is in the genetically determined chemistry of the brain, especially the primitive part of the brain called the limbic system. The limbic system is responsible for emotional behavior—the way people feel— by generating "gut reactions," the most powerful drives, behaviors, and feelings, often the ones that feel beyond the control of consciousness. Deep in the limbic system are the roots of fear, aggression, lust, and pleasure.
Dean Hamer in *Living with Our Genes*

Opossums (*Didelphis marsupialis*) are the only marsupials (pouched mammals) that live in North America. Millions of years ago they probably arrived from South America. They now occupy habitats throughout the United States, except an area in the Midwest.

When an opossum is threatened, it plays dead, going into a catatonic state, head limp with mouth open, teeth exposed, tongue hanging out—even a greenish liquid oozes from an anal gland. Scientists now think that opossums aren't clever enough to devise such deceit, but rather, they faint from fright.

Opossum teaches us how to use appearances. Sometimes it is necessary to "play dead." Sometimes it is necessary to put up a particular front to succeed most easily and effectively. . . . It also can show you when others are putting up false fronts and deceptions. Opossum has an archetypal energy that helps us to use appearances to our greatest benefit and that helps us to recognize when others are creating false impressions.

Ted Andrews in *Animal-Speak*

*A*t night, **opossums** become active, foraging for beetles, butter-flies, grasshoppers, worms, lizards, frogs, small snakes, birds' eggs, seeds, berries, nuts, and pet food.

Spring mating results in females giving birth about two weeks later to as many as twenty bumblebee-sized infants. The tiny opossums crawl their way to their mother's pouch, where thirteen nipples provide milk for the most determined thirteen infants. Those who don't latch on to a nipple don't survive.

Several weeks after birth, the babies and their mother begin wandering at night, foraging for food and learning to survive on whatever food is available.

Learn to imitate Opossum and play dead, in the sense that the best strategy is no defense. In assuming the viewpoint of no defense, you have chosen the right to be who and what you are with no games involved. . . . You owe no one an excuse for how you feel or what you choose to experience.
Jamie Sams and David Carson in *Medicine Cards*

ubterranean termites (*Reticulitermes*) live in decaying roots, trees, or lumber. Similar to ants in their caste system, each termite performs a specific duty. But worker ants are all sterile females, whereas termite workers can be either sex in any caste. The system includes queens and kings, both having wings because they are the only ones who will leave the colony at certain times to mate. After they start a new community, they shed their wings, having no need to go anywhere.

Hundreds of thousands of termites function as a single entity, as if orchestrated by an outside force, but always for the best interest of the colony itself. Some termites, with the dramatic flair that insects are so good at, will self-destruct in defense of their nest mates, exploding their blood and organs all over their attackers.

It were happy if we studied Nature more in natural things, and acted according to Nature, whose rules are few, plain, and most reasonable.
William Penn in *Some Fruits of Solitude*

Grouped termites keep touching each other incessantly with their antennae....
Isolated, paired termites are something else again. As soon as they are
removed from the group, and the touching from all sides comes to an end, they
become aggressive, standoffish; they begin drinking compulsively,
and abstain from touching each other.

Lewis Thomas in *The Lives of a Cell*

*M*embers of a colony of **termites** stay familiar with each other by constantly touching, not only for identity, but to maintain the health, stability, and strength of the social structure. If you break into the log of a termite colony, you see thousands of workers, white and wingless, male and female, communicating. Soldiers, too, with their huge heads, begin sending messages of urgency. All members cater to the queen and her eggs, shown here in the middle, surrounded by (clockwise from left) soldier, worker, and winged male.

Termites can't digest the wood they eat, but little parasites living in their intestines perform that task. And, living inside *those* little creatures, are parasitic bacteria that provide the enzymes needed to break down the cellulose in the wood. Each termite is a reflection of the cooperative effort of the entire colony.

It might be said that over millions of years the termites domesticated the
microorganisms to serve their special needs. That, however,
would be big-organism chauvinism.

Edward O. Wilson in *The Diversity of Life*

One has to be very careful these days about saying, without careful qualification, that any particular behavior is inherited. So it is almost refreshing to hear that the "song pattern of each cricket species is stored in its genes," that the distinctive song patterns of the world's some three thousand cricket species are not learned, but are "encoded" in the insects' chromosomes.

Robert A. Wallace in *Animal Behavior*

Crickets sing by rubbing their wings together, unlike grasshoppers, which usually rub their hind legs against veins on their wings. Crickets' ears are on their front legs. Each ear is a flat membrane called a tympanum—similar to a human eardrum, except a cricket's is far more sensitive to sound waves. The tympanum shown here is the dark area on the enlarged leg.

Mating between crickets begins with the female approaching a male, whose identity she determines from his song. Before copulation starts, the male sings one, two, or more songs.

Then he sings the post-copulatory song (which the French, of course, call the triumphal song). This may help to keep the inseminated female around for a while so that her pregnancy is not interfered with by other males. Should one male invade the territory of another, a fierce fight ensues, which is accompanied by the aggressive song if the fight is particularly severe. The winner goes on singing this song after the loser has been booted out.

Robert A. Wallace in *Animal Behavior*

*B*lanketflowers, or **firewheels** (*Gaillardia pulchella*), are in the same family as sunflowers. Their bright orange, red, and yellow petals give them their common name, "firewheel." The radiant colors glow in the bright sunlight and stay aflame long after other wildflowers have faded.

Dr. Edward Bach, immunologist and bacteriologist, discovered that morning dew on plants exposed to sunlight absorbed healing properties more than those in the shade. He believed these *essences* promoted healing and "are able, like beautiful music or any gloriously uplifting thing which gives us inspiration, to raise our very natures and bring us nearer to ourselves and by that very act to bring us peace and relieve our suffering."

How can nature give us an insight? In a workshop I led some years ago,
I took all the participants on a walk. . . . One woman who'd been through a
tremendous number of abrupt and drastic changes throughout her life saw
only winter images: bare trees, broken limbs, dead patches of grass.
The person who walked right next to her saw daffodils and
grass shoots coming up through the soil.
Carol L. McClelland in *The Seasons of Change*

Soldier bugs are also called stink bugs because of the strong, disgusting odor they emit when threatened.

Adults of the **spiny soldier bug** (*Podisus*) emerge from the ground in early spring when food becomes available. Food is their top priority after spending months underground. Both males and females eat their way through spring's abundance of caterpillars, consuming thousands of insects and insect larvae.

During feeding orgies, stink bugs stab their victims with needle-sharp beaks and inject them with enzymes that dissolve their bodies from the inside. The stink bugs suck out the juices, leave the empty carcass, and move on to the next meal.

When a male stink bug discovers a particularly abundant buffet of caterpillars, he sends a chemical signal to spread the word to all the other hungry stink bugs. This gathering also serves as a meeting place for males and females.

A person buying products in a supermarket is in touch with his deepest emotions.
John Kenneth Galbraith

*H*ollyhocks (*Alcea rosea*) range in color from white to pink to red to violet. The darker forms are collected for pharmaceutical use; the green part of the flower helps to heal diseases of the upper respiratory tract, and tea mixtures relieve chest colds.

The genus name for hollyhocks comes from the Greek *althea,* meaning "that which heals." The grave of a human buried 60,000 years ago was found in Iraq in 1963. In the grave were several medicinal plants, including hollyhocks.

The healing potential of flowering plants is an integral part of the deep bond that exists between humans and nature. That flowers have the ability to heal us, not only physically but also emotionally and spiritually, is something that has been recognized and utilized as far back as we know.

Anne McIntyre in *Flower Power*

*Though I do not believe a plant will spring up where no seed has been,
I have great faith in a seed. Convince me that you have a seed
there, and I am prepared to expect wonders.*
Henry David Thoreau

Oak trees (*Quercus*) are some of the most widespread trees in North America and have the largest number of species—fifty-eight trees and ten bushes.

The acorns from oaks provide food in the winter when little else is available for birds, raccoons, squirrels, and deer.

A newly sprouted acorn develops strong and full-size leaves right away, giving the seedling an advantage to mature among the foragers and competitors.

*Imagine that every person is born a seed or an acorn; all their potential is
compressed in that tiny form. Whether they reach their potential as mighty oaks
depends on many factors, but they are born as unique individuals
with their own distinguishing characteristics.*
Dean Hamer in *Living with Our Genes*

The long, distinctive snout of the **acorn weevil** (*Curculio*) helps to identify this otherwise nondescript bug—but nondescript compared only with the thousands of flamboyantly colored beetles of America. Instead of flashy attire, this beetle uses her multipurpose nose to get on with life.

Chewing mouthparts at the end of her long beak are used for boring holes in acorns, into which she lays her eggs. Antennae extend from the beak about midway down, and she can fold them back into grooves like a pocketknife while she eats. The tiny holes commonly seen in acorns are probably made by the acorn weevil.

Her larvae mature inside the acorns, surrounded by food and protected from predators by the hard shell. After the acorn falls from its tree, the larvae crawl out to burrow in the ground where they spend the next one, two, or three winters.

As if on cue during the spring they pupate, maturing within their solitary case to emerge in the warmth of the summer. Each weevil-occupied acorn has two holes; one made by the mother to lay her egg, and the other by the larva to escape.

Alonetime brings forth our wishes to explore, our curiosity about the unknown, our desires to escape from another's control, our will to be an individual, our hopes for freedom. Alonetime is fuel for life.
Ester Schaler Buchholz in *The Call of Solitude*

The scientific name for **mockingbirds,** *Mimus polyglottos,* means "imitator of many languages." For some birds, songs are learned by listening to their parents and neighbors during the first year. For other birds, songs are hardwired—the music is scored in their brains from the beginning. For mockingbirds, singing is a lifetime of choir practice and talent shows, picking up new tunes and modifying old ones.

The songs of mockingbirds vary distinctly between seasons, reflecting their two main activities: sex and food. By the time chicks are born, courtship songs end, and their focus changes from reproduction to feeding. They begin to search for insect-rich territory rather than nest-appropriate trees, and their calls are used as signals of food or as territorial warnings.

Mockingbirds flare their wings while scurrying on the ground, exposing bright white patches to attract insects. The action exposes insects, which the mockers snatch as fast as the insects become visible.

For have you not perceived that imitations, whether of bodily gestures, tones of voice, or modes of thought, if they be persevered in from an early age, are apt to grow into habits and a second nature?

Plato

The urgent calls of the **gray catbird** (*Dumetella carolinensis*) signal the activity of spring, when birds and insects—typically quiet through the winter—suddenly find their voices. The insistent urges to reproduce bring on mating calls and scurrying to build nests.

The catlike mewing gives the catbird its name, but they also make up songs as they go along, possibly mocking others, and improvising with no apparent agenda—no two songs are alike—as if they're covering as much musical ground as possible to rouse any sluggard who still lingers in winter.

Catbirds are one of the first spring arrivals, often when snow is still on the ground, as if eager to end their perfunctory show of migration and anxious to get on with their busybody chores of spring.

The change from storm and winter to serene and mild weather, from dark and sluggish hours to bright and elastic ones, is a memorable crisis which all things proclaim. It is seemingly instantaneous at last.
Henry David Thoreau

The first line of defense is a bird's song, which essentially means:
Here I am, females welcome, males keep off.
Bruce Brooks in *On the Wing*

𝒯he reputation of the maligned **blue jay** (*Cyanocitta cristata*) is largely dramatized. Humans register the raucous screams of their calls because they happen to be the loudest among the *neighborhood* birds—certainly not as loud as some of the forest woodpeckers or as intrusive as the smaller starlings—while their softer, gentler nature goes unnoticed. Often, humans don't recognize the jays' subtle cooing as a male brings his mate food. Simple calls between pairs during incubation are muffled in the thick tangle of their nest habitat and the mating calls of other species.

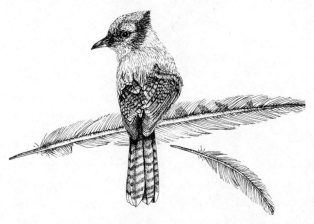

I studied under Grandpa Fools Crow, a Lakota holy man. He said never
bad-mouth anybody, never be envious or jealous of anybody; if you are,
you won't be on the right road yourself, 'cause all roads are good.
Abe Conklin in *All Roads Are Good*

Scrub habitat is sandy, low, dry, gnarled, and weedy. When asked, "Why bother saving this dried up old scrub?" Florida scrub researcher Dr. John Fitzpatrick answered, "Why save the *Mona Lisa*? It's old and doesn't produce anything for us either.... Scrub is a gold mine of genetic information. These are plants that have spent a million years evolving ways to deal with a very specialized problem: hot, wet summers, cool, dry winters, poor soil—all things that humans have to deal with."

Two isolated groups of **scrub jays** (*Aphelocoma coerulescens*) exist in the United States, separated from each other by the vast mid United States. A large population lives in the woods of a few western states including California, Arizona, and Colorado, and a small isolated group lives in a narrow ridge of Florida. Separated by a thousand miles, the birds are similar, but the Florida scrub jay has a white line above the eyes and a frosted forehead, lacking on the western scrub jays.

*Scrub is subtle, gnarled, sometimes impenetrable. Scrub is glare and prickle.
Its plants are clothed in the khaki of camouflage; its animals are dry-skinned
and fossorial. Its shaman is the sky-blue scrub jay, and there is no
green more hopeful than the scrub oak in springtime.*
Susan Cerulean of the Florida Game and
Fresh Water Fish Commission

*Fatherly and motherly hearts often beat warm and wise in the breasts
of bachelor uncles and maiden aunts; and it is my private opinion that these
worthy creatures are a beautiful provision of nature for the
cherishing of other people's children.*
Louisa May Alcott

Scrub jays in Florida are friendly toward humans and will readily land on heads, arms, and hands. They live only in scrub habitat—dry and high— the same type of land that humans use to build homes. Humans, more aggressive and stronger than the gentle bird, have replaced the scrub jay in the majority of scrub habitat. Unlike the more adaptable blue jays, scrub jays can't exist without their scrub habitat.

Unlike almost any other bird, scrub jays live in tight social communities with small family groups of half a dozen or so. Pairs mate for life, and their offspring become "helpers," staying within their clan for several years. Each family member has its place in the structure, even uncles, who will, when necessary, replace deceased males. Different members take turns as sentries, guarding members and issuing warnings if a hawk or invasive blue jay approaches.

*You white people are so strange. We think it is very primitive
for a child to have only two parents.*
Australian Aboriginal elder

*F*ifteen species of **dogwoods** (*Cornus*) grow in the United States, and although we mostly think of them as trees, they also grow as shrubs and wildflowers.

A popular tree among wildlife, its bark, twigs, and berries are all used as health aids, including the twigs as a toothbrush with ground bark as toothpaste. Birds and mammals eat the fruit. Insects use the bark for mating, eating, and burrowing.

Flowering dogwoods, shown here with buds, bloom in April and May, attracting many neighborhood and backyard birds such as evening grosbeaks, cardinals, cedar waxwings, and wood thrushes.

*I like trees because they seem more resigned to the
way they have to live than other things.*
Willa Cather

*E*arthworms (*Lumbricus terrestris*) live in underground burrows in moist soil and dig their way through the earth in search of food. As they forage, the soil is aerated and fertilized. Birds, centipedes, insects, and slugs follow the worms, creating more tilling. This in turn allows rain-water and air to seep into tunnels and crevices, enriching the soil.

Earthworms feed on bits of leaves and roots, which they also preserve and store by coating each particle with digestive juices, then packing it into their burrows. Dirt eaten with the food is ground in their gizzards, adding a fine soil to the earth when they pass the digested food through their intestines. Tiny mud balls are excreted in piles just outside their burrows. Aristotle called earthworms the "guts of the soil."

It may be doubted if there are any other animals
which have played such an important part of history of the world
as these lowly organized creatures.
Charles Darwin

Earthworms have no eyes but can sense approaching danger by picking up soil vibrations from birds, moles, shrews, snakes, salamanders, and toads. To avoid being pulled from their burrow, they anchor themselves to the walls by extending tiny, stiff bristles into the soil.

Strictly nocturnal, they remain in their burrows through the day, only poking their head out at night. Spring rains often flush earthworms out of their burrow. Since worms have no sense of direction, they can't find their way back, even when their burrow is only an inch away. The dried worms that we see shriveled on the sidewalks have simply lost their way.

A good sense of direction is hereditary. Some animals travel using tiny particles embedded in their brain tissue to orient themselves magnetically. Many animals, including worms and some humans, didn't receive that inheritance, so we spend a lot of time figuring out where we are. According to many neurologists, getting lost is a form of dyslexia, biologically determined.

Most people think of dyslexia as the simple tendency to flip letters and symbols with a few right-left problems thrown in. It's nowhere near that simple. . . . I've found that nobody has a good theory of what causes it. . . . Most dyslexics learn to live with it on their own. They avoid what they can't do, think of alternate ways to do what they need to do . . . until the next dyslexic moment hits.
Mark Lane in "Dyslexics of the World Untie!" in
June 9, 1996, *News-Journal* (Daytona, Florida)

During mating, **earthworms** secrete a milky fluid trail that helps them find mates. Each worm has both male and female sex organs; two worms simply exchange sperm with each other. They clasp each other tightly, belly to belly, using bristles and slime to stick together, sometimes for the entire night.

A mucus tube is formed during this coupling by a special gland called a *clitellum*, which later becomes a ring and separates from each worm. This segment, filled with eggs and sperm, is left in the soil, where the fertilized eggs develop into worms. The egg cases, often dug up by gardeners, are yellowish, lemon-shaped capsules about the size of an apple-seed.

An earthworm's life, as an egg and as an adult, is spent almost entirely surrounded by soil. For many humans, wide-open spaces are as frightening as tight spots are for claustrophobics. Those of us with this kind of inheritance know the primal security of blankets, small rooms, and cozy clusters of people nearby. People of this nature wouldn't survive in isolated ranch houses or wide-open prairies.

Pressure over wide areas of the body has a calming effect on many animals. . . .
I decided to try the squeeze chute and discovered that the intense pressure
temporarily made my anxiety go away. When I returned home
from the ranch I built a squeezing machine. . . .
Temple Grandin in "Thinking Like Animals,"
from *Intimate Nature*

Singing among birds is usually done by males, but among **bluebirds** (*Sialia*), both male and female sing. The male songbird sings during courtship to impress a female, but also to give her information about his genetic background. Is the female bluebird simply providing information? During nesting, partners are known to change mates between broods, their songs continuing through the summer to inform, warn, or locate each other.

The expectant silence after a bluebird's call is as meaningful as the pauses in between human conversations, and the range of notes and accents provides the ability to communicate far beyond human senses.

Using *only twenty-six letters,* humans can write about medicine, history, biology, electronics, dreams, food, fashion, feelings ... but birds have a range of notes equivalent to our alphabet—and probably more. God only knows all the information *they* exchange.

> *Some birds are poets and sing all summer. They are the true singers.*
> *Any man can write verses during the love season.*
> Henry David Thoreau

*More than at any other time, we feel the strangeness of birds when we stop and
pick up a feather in our path. There is nothing on Earth to compare it to;
there is no material like it, no form, nothing
that functions quite the same way.*

Bruce Brooks in *On the Wing*

To look at a **feather** through a magnifying glass is to see a miracle in engineering, art, and evolution. Each feather
has hundreds of barbules interlocking with one
another to form a seal as protective as any
mammal's fur or any reptile's scales.

Feathers lock in warmth, keep out
moisture, create flight, show sex, tell age,
and blend into backgrounds. Feathers can
also *change* the way a bird looks—miraculously, according to the owner's need.
Stripes, dots, solids, swirls, and her-
ringbones; each feather has its own
design, its own identity—and its
own purpose. Each season millions of
feathers are lost by their owners with no
more fanfare than a tree dropping a leaf.

*Not all birds fly, or sing, or build nests. Yet all birds share one feature: feathers.
No bird lacks them or can survive without them.*

Maryjo Koch in *Bird Egg Feather Nest*

*To guarantee their survival, the genes found a clever trick. Instead of
appealing to our higher sense of calling, or our duty to continue the human race,
the genes made sex feel good, real good.*

Dean Hamer in *Living with Our Genes*

Mating in the animal kingdom is not solely for reproduction. **Kestrels** (*Falco sparverius*) may mate five
hundred to seven hundred times for one clutch of
eggs.

For a few months during courtship, breeding,
and incubation, male and female kestrels have
marked divisions of chores; the female always stays near the nest,
while the male stalks his hunting
grounds for food, which he
brings to his mate. This routine of
hunting-receiving begins long before incubation, while the female is
still able to hunt for herself.

*In the avian world, foreplay lasts much longer than sex.
While the actual act of insemination takes place in a matter of seconds,
courtship rituals can occupy days or even weeks. This slow process of bonding
has a definite purpose: it not only establishes connections,
it engenders trust in normally solitary birds.*

Sharon A. Cohen in *Bird Nests*

_____

April comes like an idiot, babbling, and strewing flowers.
Edna St. Vincent Millay

Common fleabanes (*Erigeron philadelphicus*) have asterlike white or pink petals with yellow centers. They bloom in April, their bright flowers standing out among the rough brown weeds and leaf litter in fields and lots, where they commonly grow.

Colors and scents in flowers are signals to insect pollinators. Flowers, which were a later development of plants over the past millions of years, were at first dependent on the fickleness of wind for reproduction—how does a flower reproduce when it can't *go* anywhere? It entices insects to do the work of carrying pollen, getting their attention first by advertising. Millions of years later, this still works.

There is such intelligence to creation, such power of generation that humans have had few spare ways to understand it, express it, or connect with it except through religion and art and more recently, science, which now seems to border on a thin "cutting" edge with a sometimes hard objectivity on one side, the mystical and the miraculous on the other.
Linda Hogan in "First People," from *Intimate Nature*

*I*n the spring, butterflies are attracted to the bright clusters of flowers of **lantanas** (*Lantana involucrata*). The close arrangement of small flowers provides an easy area for landing and a large surface for perching. In addition, the butterfly doesn't have to use a lot of energy flying from one to the next, since dozens of little nectar pots are conveniently next to each other.

Lantanas are common in waste areas in the south—surprisingly beautiful growing next to weeds in sandy fields and along the sides of roads, as if they were nothing special.

If spring means the coming of summer, it likewise represents the fading of winter. It is a passing away. There are spring departures as well as arrivals. . . . Nature has asserted its superiority to politics. We are confronted with the majesty of a truth . . . we cannot help but see how even the greatest among us is still subject to the same cycle of life as the fish in the pond or the flower in the sand.

Louis J. Halle in "Spring in Washington"

in *The American Year*

Every spring, according to their internal clock, **garden snails** (*Helix pomatia*) begin a complex ritual of foreplay and mating to exchange sperm.

Equipped with both male and female organs, they approach each other for mating, cautiously testing, not so much for sex recognition but to make sure the other is the right species. After a slow and slippery dance of gentle touching, they will suddenly shoot each other with sharp love darts—perhaps to test the authenticity of the potential sperm donor or, according to many researchers, to simply increase stimulation. If they both survive and aren't seriously wounded, they continue on to swap sperm, which each stores until later in the summer.

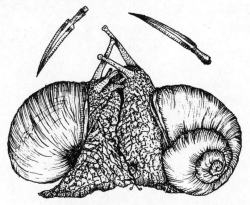

Because we prize reason and are confused about our biology, we refer to our body's cravings and demands as our "baser" motives, instincts, or drives. So it is craven to yearn for sex, but noble to yearn for music, for example.
Diane Ackerman in *A Natural History of Love*

Gray squirrels (*Silvilagus carolinensis*) race up and down poles, trees, and fences with incredible speed by using their strong feet and toes. Their front paws have four toes for holding nuts and seeds, but their back feet have five toes, enabling them to go down trees headfirst by hooking all five claws firmly into bark and wood. (House cats can climb *up* a tree easily but have trouble getting down.) Also giving them agility and speed are ankles that can swivel, allowing them to turn, leap, and push from their position as no other mammal can.

Rarely do squirrels stay still. Even when not running, their tails are moving and their faces are twitching. Their entire body always seems to be vibrating.

front feet

hind feet

The erratic behavior of Squirrel has bested many a forlorn hunter, and it thus stands to reason that there are benefits to being able to circle a branch at lightning speed. This erratic behavior of Squirrel can also get nerve-wracking if you are dealing with persons who have Squirrel medicine. Trying to calm them down enough to accomplish something may drive you nuts.

Jamie Sams and David Carson in *Medicine Cards*

Mating among **squirrels** begins with wild, high-energy chases up and over branches, bushes, trees, and logs. They build large, loose nests in trees, made from leaves, branches, and twigs, where the babies remain as hairless blobs of gray flesh until they have matured into almost fully grown adults with bushy tails.

Their fluffy tails are used to distract predators—flicking it will draw attention to the tail, which the predator will attack, rather than the soft, vulnerable body.

Without those fluffy tails, squirrels would look like rats—they survive so well in urban areas by virtue of their cuteness.

Squirrels can teach us balance within the circle of gathering and giving out. . . .
Squirrels are the masters at preparing, but they also are reminders that in
our quest for our goals, we should always make time to socialize
and play. Work and play go hand-in-hand, or the work will create
problems and become more difficult and less fruitful.
Ted Andrews in *Animal-Speak*

Gray squirrels are active during the day, racing, eating, storing, tumbling, and climbing. Hours each day are spent storing food, hiding nuts and seeds in crevices in trees and underground hiding places.

In addition to storing food for later, they overeat at certain times to develop fat deposits. Prior to hibernation, the brain stops its normal "I'm full" signal mechanism. When the stomach is full, the squirrel continues to eat, driven by a survival instinct to stay alive through hibernation. Even though food will likely be available in the winter, genetically they are programmed to hide enough food to last through a famine.

We are carrying the fat of the land on our swelling bodies. Much of the problem is the result of our success as a species. We have conquered nature and divided our labors so that some people never have to lift a finger to survive.

Dean Hamer in *Living with Our Genes*

Ground squirrels (*Citellus*) live in dens and burrows, and unlike the active tree life of gray squirrels, they forage, eat, and communicate with each other on the ground.

Squirrels communicate by changing the pitch and loudness of their chirps and clicks. They also use their tails and body gestures to let other squirrels know danger is near or trespassers are approaching.

Like most hibernating mammals, ground squirrels are seen less and less as winter approaches, slowing down and eventually going underground after many long, active months of mating, building nests, raising young, eating, and storing food. Similar to many mammals, including humans, fewer hours of light trigger chemical responses to retreat and conserve energy.

The origins of the influences of light on our activity are rooted far back in the evolutionary past. The survival of our species has depended on matching the workings of our bodies and minds to the demands of the day and night.
Winifred Gallagher in *The Power of Place*

*F*lying squirrels (*Glaucomys volans*) are actually *gliding* squirrels; the wide flaps on their sides are not true wings but allow them to slow down as they jump from their treetop positions. The tail is used as a rudder to guide their direction, but any flight distance is covered only during the descent.

All North American squirrels are active during the day, except flying squirrels. Their evolutionary departure from ground-dwelling animals led them to living high up in treetops, safe from predators below.

Rodents that live in trees are more high-strung than ground dwellers. They can never sleep as soundly, since the sudden approach of winds or storm activity may threaten their safety. Flying squirrels kept as pets become nervous and restless during storms.

This is an otherwise rather dumpy, stubby little rodent that has, for no good reason, wings. It's as though nature gave the squirrel wings casually, for fun, with the randomness of a bright child drawing horns and mustachios on people in magazines to make a rainy day pass. Let's see what this guy looks like with an elephant nose. Let's make this one fly.
Castle Freeman, Jr., in *Spring Snow*

The stinger of a **honeybee** (*Apis mellifera*) has poison glands with sharp barbs that remain in the victim, continuing to pump venom through the skin—hence, the long-term pain.

Even though they can inflict a painful jab, honeybees are more interested in finding nectar than stinging a human. They attack when threatened, but only as a last defense. With the injection, their stinger and venom sac are ripped from their body and they die. When threatened, they first send signals to their nest mates, who typically swarm to the caller's defense immediately.

Honeybee members communicate with chemicals, dancing, buzzes, and emphatic gesturing. When a worker bee returns to her colony, her hive mates first frisk her to make sure she's not a spy or invader. After she proves that she's not an imposter, she describes her afternoon adventures with complex body gestures. The detailed charades describe exact distance and direction to a new food source, potential danger, and quality and abundance of available food.

There has been a genuine change in our perception of animal behavior brought about by detailed studies of animals that have revealed far more complexity than was previously imagined. And because this change is a relatively recent one, it has not yet filtered through to the outside world, and is not yet fully reflected in the views of those who are tempted to dismiss all non-human animals as necessarily simple or stupid.

Marian Stamp Dawkins in *Through Our Eyes Only?*

𝓑umblebees (*Bombus*) have huge bodies, much larger than honeybees, with relatively small wings that seem too small to carry all their weight. But they fly in between grasses and plants, zigzagging with a bumbling determination, eventually probing deep into blossoms with their long tongues, collecting nectar that honeybees can't reach.

Queens are the loudest and biggest of the bumblers, weaving in between low growth to locate a nest site. Unlike honeybees, their nests are near or in the ground, and well camouflaged. Already established nests are often taken over by strong queens who either kill the resident queen or make her submissive.

As they fly around flowers collecting food for the nest, bumblebees adjust the frequency of their buzz, changing it until the vibration is exactly right to shake the pollen from the flower. The pollen is carried away on their hind legs to be dropped at the next flower. This courier service is in exchange for the nectar the bumblebee needs.

Aerodynamically the bumblebee shouldn't be able to fly, but the bumblebee doesn't know it so it goes on flying.
Mary Kay Ash

For centuries people have eaten **propolis,** sometimes called bee glue, to boost their immune systems. Now scientists are discovering its use as an antibiotic, as protective for humans as it was for the bees.

Bees gather the sap that oozes from some plants, and they mix it with their own fluids and enzymes to make propolis. The bees use the mixture as a glue to seal the openings in their hives. The sticky goo discourages intruders from entering; if they should trespass, they will likely become trapped in the substance.

The busy-as-a-bee cliché doesn't do justice to a bee's talent for doing nothing. As much as we think *all* bees are *always* collecting pollen, making honey, smearing propolis, and serving their queen, they actually spend the better part of their day resting.

[We] might do well to consider that laziness is perfectly natural, perfectly sensible, and is shared by nearly every other species on the planet.
Natalie Angier in *The Beauty of the Beastly*

Queen **honeybees** fly far and high to mate with
drones. The strongest and fastest of these males
are the ones who reach her, and she collects
sperm from the best of the best—enough to
last a lifetime of egg-laying. The male, having
injected his genitalia into her, dies from the
detachment—not a problem in nature however, since his genes are guaranteed to
continue—his organ has, in essence,
blocked her from being able to mate
with anyone else.

The queen bee, shown here, finds
her way back to her hive after mating and
begins laying as many as two thousand eggs
each day. Sometimes, however, a queen is ban-
ished when a newly hatched queen takes over.
The replaced queen is led from the hive by an
escort of workers whose allegiance is now with
their new queen. If any of the old queen's eggs remain
in the nest, the new queen cuts them open and stings the unborns
to death. If two or more queens emerge at the same time, they
fight each other until the stronger wins. The loser is killed.

*The fierceness of female friendships and the unease with which we regard other
women are in my view related phenomena, and are the legacy of dissonance
between our ancient primate and our neohominid selves and of our inherent
strategic plasticity, the desire to keep all options open. Other females are a
potential source of strength, and other females can destroy us.*
Natalie Angier in *Woman: An Intimate Geography*

April 13

A **honeybee** colony can have 30,000 to 60,000 members. The hexagonal cells of a honeycomb hold the honey, pollen, and brood for the colony. Each wax cell is constructed pointing slightly upward so the honey doesn't spill out. They are built by workers who serve their queen.

Both queens and workers are female. Which one they become is determined by what they eat as larvae. Young queen larvae are fed special royal jelly. The ones who become workers then build the special chambers and never lay eggs. The queen spends her day laying eggs, which are tended by other members of the colony. The fertilized eggs become females, and the unfertilized become males.

The relationships among the colonizers seem planned with an elegance of balance and acceptance that succeeds from one generation to the next.

Drones are treated like sex objects, useful only in copulation. The females live,
but they live only to work. They tend the queen, rear the young, and
maintain and defend the hive. And they literally wear themselves
out in their service . . . but the hive goes on.
Robert A. Wallace in *Animal Behavior*

*H*oneybees have magnetic compounds in certain tissues in their bodies. These concentrated compounds act as compasses, allowing the bees to use Earth's magnetic field. The same magnetic compounds are found in some birds and mammals, ensuring the travelers will always find their way home.

A communications network of honeybees consists of reporters, receivers, translators, messengers, and analysts. Receiver bees, always at the hive, collect all the information from the many reporters who return to the nest with the news of the day. By performing a complex dance, they report new food spots and potential real estate possibly needed for future expansion.

At times, a queen flies from her old hive to start a new colony. Over a period of a few days, her swarm mates search for possible sites for her. Using the show-and-tell method, each agent reports her real-estate details—location, sun exposure, safety, privacy, and accessibility to food, drink, and supplies.

Put people with "place talents" in a new city, and they immediately know how to get to the museums. Others cannot tell their left from their right or identify where north and west are.
Robert Ornstein in *The Roots of the Self*

Red clover (*Trifolium pratense*) is one of those roadside and lawn flowers that always seems to have bees buzzing around it. Everything about them is made to attract insects to come to them—color, size, shape, and scent.

Bumblebees buzz around the clover flower until they find the opening to the nectar. To get to it, they must struggle to get inside the narrow entrance, which triggers the pistil. This, in turn, springs up to collect the pollen on the bee's head from a previously visited clover. Then, the stamen springs up, covering the bee's head with its own pollen.

The most beautiful thing we can experience is the mysterious. It is the source of all true art and science. He to who this emotion is a stranger, who can no longer pause to wonder and stand rapt in awe, is as good as dead: his eyes are closed.
Albert Einstein

Black and white warblers (*Mniotilta varia*) are also known as black and white creepers because of their habit of creeping along the bark of trees and tree trunks looking for trunk-dwelling insects and bark-camouflaged moths. As if guided, black and white warblers migrate to areas where insects are abundant.

It is one of the first birds to arrive at their nesting grounds, after migrating from their winter home—as far as South America. The spring migration begins as early as February, and many southern states see the warblers at the end of the winter en route to their northern nesting areas.

In Spring, timing is everything. A flock of birds migrating north before the last winter storm may have to put up quite a struggle just to survive; seedlings coming up before the last frost have to be very hardy in order to withstand the harsh conditions. Most animals and plants have an internal sense that tells them when it's safe to venture forth and pursue spring activities.
Carol L. McClelland in *The Seasons of Change*

Cerulean warblers (*Dendroica cerulea*) are more difficult to spot than some of the other wood warblers, camouflaged neatly high up in treetops—males are sky blue and females are blue-gray above, and leafy green below.

Males arrive at the nesting areas between April and May, depending on how far north they fly, and females arrive about two weeks later. The males begin singing when they arrive and continue until the females join them.

Nesting begins with constructing an intricate nest made from grass, fibers, feathers, moss, hair, and vines, all bound by attaching bark with spider silk. Cocoons are added to the outside, possibly as camouflage, or perhaps just as an added artistic flourish. Throughout the building process, females leave the nests to gather materials by jumping, bungee-cord style, then dropping straight down until an abrupt U-turn ends their dramatic leap.

During her foraging, she picks up any available stick, leaf, or fiber, then tests it for fit; if it works, she tucks it in securely—if it doesn't work, she lets it go—and selects another piece. The haphazard placement of twigs and leaves is a sturdy, interlocking arrangement—its very irregularity not only disguises it among the branches, but gives it a durability created from millions of years of experience.

To live a creative life, we must lose our fear of being wrong.
Joseph Chilton Pearce

What's the difference between a true **songbird** and a singing bird? The anatomy of songbirds is different from other birds, even from those that sing. Songbirds have more muscles in their music-making throats, and their wings and feet are structured so they can position themselves on a branch to properly belt out a tune.

Songbirds also differ from other songsters by learning their scores from parents and neighbors, as opposed to birds whose repertoires are innate, that is, hardwired in their brains. To process the stages of learning tunes, the brains of songbirds are necessarily larger than other birds.

Not only are their songs highly complex, their nest-building techniques are sophisticated and intricate. Weaving, knotting, and decorating with shells, feathers, fibers, flowers, and string is not unusual for songbirds, and their nests are creations worthy of any blue ribbon.

I want to sing like birds sing . . . not worrying
who hears or what they think.

Rumi

April 19

*All that a man has to say or do that can possibly concern mankind,
is in some shape or other to tell the story of his love—to sing; and if he is
fortunate and keeps alive, he will be forever in love.*
Henry David Thoreau

The great variety of sounds from **song-birds** has evolved partly from the differences in their surroundings: noise in forests travels differently from noise in open prairies.

Sound waves, according to their frequencies, are amplified or reduced depending on a range of factors including the size of nearby trees, denseness of leaves, temperature, soil texture, and air pollution. How can one little bird create a recognizable sound while competing with a forest having its own orchestra of insects, frogs, streams, rustling leaves, falling branches, growls from mammals, and *thousands of other birds?*

And through all this, how does a small bird make a sound loud enough for a female to select him over all the other males—but not so loud that an enemy will hear? It's a wonder that we have any songsters at all, let alone the millions that sing through the day as if it were no big deal.

*Many guys have come to you
With a line that wasn't true
And you passed them by . . .
Why don't you let me try . . .
All I know is lalalalalalalala means I love you.*
"La La (Means I Love You)" by Thom Bell and William Hart

Although mated pairs are common among **indigo buntings** (*Passerina cyanea*), females are known to be promiscuous. Promiscuity is a general term used to describe bird behavior when they mate with more than one partner, and it does not imply morality. We call animal behavior "natural" when it's something we like, but "animalistic" when it's an activity that makes us uncomfortable.

A female necessarily invests more time and energy into raising offspring than does the male. If her mate is a bad investment in genes, she can increase her chance of raising healthy and strong chicks with a variety of sperm. Because promiscuous males and females produce more offspring, their genes are more likely to survive.

Lest there be any remaining sentimentality about monogamy in birds, recent studies of two classically territorial and supposedly monogamous birds—white-crowned sparrows and indigo buntings—should settle the matter. . . . Researchers have found that a whopping 34 percent of white-crowned sparrow young were not the offspring of the putative father. About the same level of illicit conception was found in buntings.
Jake Page and Eugene S. Morton in *Lords of the Air*

Why don't birds fall out of trees when they're sleeping? When birds "sit" on branches, tendons in the legs pull their claws into a closed position and lock the birds onto their perch. When awake, the bird "stands," unlocking the tendons to prepare to take off.

Most backyards with feeders attract **cardinals** (*Cardinalis cardinalis*). Cardinals forage, court, nest, and feed chicks—all within human viewing distance, as the nests are usually less than ten feet from the ground. Many pairs breed twice a year, and both parents are active in raising the chicks. A male brings gifts of food to his mate—an indication of his "earning capacity." His gifts reflect rank, strength, and an ability to protect his family.

When a male and female finally get together, the female chases the male around, pecks him painfully, he pecks back, and they engage in a kind of spat before she accepts him. They will end up mating and rearing offspring, but why bother with the squabbling? Unless it is a way for her to test him, to make sure that he'll be a faithful and devoted father even when the going gets rough, as it's bound to once the chicks arrive.
Do human lovers have spats for the same reason?
Diane Ackerman in *A Slender Thread*

Puffing up her feathers and squeaking, she looks helpless and cold, but actually she's inviting her mate to court. Though acting like a hungry infant bird, she is perfectly able to feed herself, and will. This dramatic appeal is the time-honored way that female cardinals (and many other birds) play house. . . . I shake my head and sigh. I'm ashamed to admit it, but from time to time human females can act just as infantile when a male is around. . . .

Diane Ackerman in *A Slender Thread*

$\mathcal{A}$ female **cardinal** teaches her mate how to recognize feeding signals of their future chicks by acting like a baby herself—since both parents feed the chicks, the female "trains" her mate to respond to a hungry chick. While she is nest-bound, sitting on the second set of eggs, the male continues to bring food to her while still caring for the first brood.

An increased parental role for males may well have become essential because the females . . . could not bear the full costs of child care while foraging on their own. . . . It must have been at this point that the unusually intense pair-bonding that occurs between human males and females first evolved.

Robin Dunbar in *Grooming, Gossip, and the Evolution of Language*

Zinnias (*Zinnia*) grow in every color except blue. They thrive in heat and will stay in bloom throughout the summer. It's known as the "youth and old age" flower because the old flowers stay fresh even after new ones bloom.

Why do plants grow better with music? Leaves have openings, called stomata, which "breathe" the air around them. This action of air exchange is increased with particular music. Michael Holz, a musician who worked with plants, noticed that these certain songs mimicked birdsong.

[Michael Holz] began to examine the electronic frequencies and amplitudes of the music and birdsong. He discovered that birdsong was the perfect frequency and amplitude to cause stomata to increase their action to the highest level. The singing of birds, developed over millennia in the ecosystem, helped plants to grow.

Stephen Harrod Buhner in *Sacred Plant Medicine*

The cause of most common allergies is plant **pollen.** Hay fever is neither caused by hay nor does it cause fever. It's from the irritation of microscopic plant particles that travel for miles with breezes.

The shapes, sizes, and designs of pollen grains are as varied as flowers, ranging from smooth globes to spiked disks to ruffled domes.

Mucous membranes in our nose usually stop allergens like pollen from entering our system, but some people are susceptible to the invasion of these foreign objects, causing itching and sneezing. Different noses respond to the chemicals and shapes of different pollens.

When the first simple flower bloomed on some raw upland late in the Dinosaur Age, it was wind-pollinated, just like its early pinecone relatives. It was a very inconspicuous flower because it had not yet evolved the idea of using the surer attraction of birds and insects to achieve the transportation of pollen. . . . Nevertheless, the true flower—and the seed that it produced—was a profound innovation in the world of life.
Loren Eiseley in *How Flowers Changed the World*

The Navaho have that wonderful image of what they call the pollen path.
Pollen is the life source. The pollen path is the path to the center. The Navaho
say, "Oh, beauty before me, beauty behind me, beauty to the right of me, beauty
to the left of me, beauty above me, beauty below me, I'm on the pollen path."
Joseph Campbell in *The Power of Myth*

Pollen grains are the male reproductive particles that fertilize fe-male flowers. Many flowers coordinate their daytime opening to coincide with bees' schedules.

Pollen is damaged by moisture, so many plants close at night to protect the pollen from dew. Some pollen-eating insects remain all night trapped in a closed flower.

[As bumblebees go] from one flower to another at breakneck speed, they cause
explosions all over the place, the air is full of tiny pollen clouds, and
the whole scene is strongly reminiscent of a Civil War picture
or an old Western, full of gunsmoke.
B.J.D. Meeuse in *The Story of Pollination*

---

*L*arge, shiny, and black, with two orange bands across the body and clubbed antennae, the **burying beetle** (*Nicrophorus marginatus*) is commonly found in fields and woods. Why don't we notice these outlandish beetles more? Most of their time is spent underground during the day—they only emerge at night to forage.

These beetles search for dying and dead animals, especially mice and small birds, whose bodies will be used as nurseries for the beetle's offspring. Their highly sensitive odor detectors can locate a dead animal from miles away.

After finding a dead body, the beetle looks for a mate to help bury the body and begin the mating process. To find a female, the male signals with a powerful odor, which the female receives from far off. Once they get together, they bury the animal and encase it with a thick glue to protect it from rotting. They mate on the carcass and the female lays her eggs in it.

Parents are devoted to their offspring, and by the time the larvae hatch, both parents have prepared for the birth by chewing from the dead animal and then feeding the partially digested food to the immature beetles. The offspring eat, baby-bird style, with gaping mouths into which the parents spit the chewed food.

> *The world is full of signals that we don't perceive. Tiny creatures live in a different world of unfamiliar forces. . . . What an imperceptive lot we are. Surrounded by so much, so fascinating and so real, that we do not see (hear, smell, touch, taste) in nature . . .*
> Stephen Jay Gould in *The Panda's Thumb*

*K*nown as nest parasites, **brown-headed cowbirds** (*Molothrus ater*) regularly put their eggs in the nests of other birds including robins, waxwings, blue jays, thrashers, orioles, catbirds, thrushes, doves, blackbirds, goldfinches, warblers, and vireos. Most will recognize the imposter eggs and toss them out, but some birds raise the cowbird chicks as their own, even as the chick grows much larger than the foster parent, as shown here.

The cowbird chick not only grows *faster* than its nest mates, it starts growing *sooner* because the cowbird's incubation period is shorter— smaller chicks are quickly forced out of the overcrowded nest and the foster parents then devote their feeding schedule to this enormous, demanding, and uninvited guest.

The substitute parents are duped by their inflexible nurturing instincts to react to the sight of a gaping red mouth. Baby animals, including humans, have certain traits in common: proportionately larger heads, shorter limbs, bigger eyes, smaller mouths and noses—all contribute to a response to love and nurture the infant.

Occasionally a mother cowbird comes to the foster nest and feeds her own bird.
Such behavior suggests that the cowbird retains the maternal instinct and
enjoys her young so long as someone else bears the responsibility.
Sarita Van Vleck in *Ways of the Bird*

*C*owbirds often use nests of the **yellow warbler** (*Dendroica petechia*) to lay their own eggs—but when the cowbird eggs are discovered, the mother warbler builds a second nest on top. This destroys the cowbird eggs, but also destroys her own. The warbler will repeat the process as many times as necessary until the cowbird moves on.

After summer nesting is complete and chicks are grown, more than an estimated 5 billion land birds representing 187 species leave their northern homes for tropical areas. Many small birds like the yellow warbler fly at night to avoid predators. For humans to witness their migration is difficult—tiny specks in a night sky, thousands of feet high, flying on their own timetable.

Seeing how warblers migrate between breeding and winter territories at appropriate times is a humbling realization. Would that a human were free and able to travel when the urge strikes.

In the spring, billions return, many flying over the Gulf of Mexico to enter the States with tailwinds helping their journey. Many never make it, or are forced to land because of rain, fog, exhaustion, or starvation.

Among the greatest puzzles and wonders of natural history are the long and circuitous routes of migration followed by many animals. Some lengthy movements make sense as direct paths to favorable climates from season to season; they are no more peculiar than the annual winter migration to Florida of large mammals inside metallic birds.
Stephen Jay Gould in *The Panda's Thumb*

Purple martins (*Progne subis*) are the largest of the swallows, and every spring, as predictable as their Capistrano relatives, they return from South America to places where they've nested before. They often use human-built bird condominiums or hollowed-out gourds as housing, a tradition started centuries ago by Native Americans for community peace and good luck.

Nesting is a complex affair of signaling and scheduling. Polygamous instincts are generally tempered because of the timing of raising the chicks: after two months of feeding and caring for their young, the devoted parents begin their return flight to South America. Loner males often try their luck against defensive males, but do so early in the game—or else they won't have time to raise their offspring to maturity.

Purple Martins are past masters at adultery. These days, Martins usually nest in "apartment buildings" people put up in the vain hope that the birds will eat hordes of mosquitoes. Older, more experienced males arrive early in the spring. Once established in the penthouse suites (the hardest for predators to reach), they sing a dawn song that attracts younger males to the colony. Then the older birds force themselves on the younger birds' mates.
Ronald Orenstein in *Songbirds*

My body is a storehouse for my memories, a sensitive radar kit which warns me of danger, a wise teacher who signals me how best to care for my spirit.

Julia Cameron in *Blessings*

*P*eregrine comes from the Latin word for "wandering" or "coming from afar." **Peregrine falcons** are the epitome of wanderers, migrating great distances to their nesting areas each spring.

The urge to wander for many humans is dismissed or mostly ignored—but who knows what ancient longings stir within the cells of our body?

The world is full of people who have stopped listening to themselves or have listened only to their neighbors to learn what they ought to do, how they ought to behave, and what the values are that they should be living for.

Joseph Campbell

What you need you attract like a lover.
Gertrude Stein

All the features of a **peregrine falcon** are designed for hunting. In addition to their speed while flying, their eyes are proportionately large and set toward the front of the head, giving them superior vision. The sharp notch on the curved beak is used for killing prey, and their talons are long, sharp, and strong.

During the early spring nesting, the hunting skills of nesting peregrines are critical for the survival of their young. When smaller migrants arrive at their nesting grounds, exhausted at the end of their journey, they are the most vulnerable to attack by larger birds such as peregrines.

Songbirds typically travel at night, not only because of cooler temperatures, but to avoid hawks dominating the daytime skies—however, expectant peregrines are strategically placed to greet the arrival of thousands of the small birds. The timing ensures abundant food for the nesting peregrine parents and their chicks—a feast arriving daily.

No one looks twice at a sparrow or squirrel, or even once at a dandelion,
but a peregrine falcon or mountain lion is a lifetime experience.
And not just because of their size (think of a cow) or ferocity
(think of a house cat), but because they are rare.
Edward O. Wilson in *The Diversity of Life*

---

*If birds had the avian equivalent of a singles bar, it would undoubtedly
be the leks or arenas where male birds gather to parade their physical attributes
in front of the females who come to have their eggs fertilized.*

Lester L. Short in *The Lives of Birds*

𝒜 **lek** is a place where males gather during mating season and
engage in competitive displays to attract
females. They strut around
for all they're worth
to catch a female's
attention. Peacocks are the most notorious
because of their flamboyant tails, but
other birds such as hummingbirds congregate in the spring to show off for females.

But why would males congregate—exposing themselves to
predation—when only a few apparently could benefit? As Robert
A. Wallace suggests in *Animal Behavior,* "the cumulative effect of a
group of displaying males might release reproductive behavior in
females more quickly than would the efforts of a single male."

*Eventually, having settled on the best of what may well be a bad bunch, each
female mates with the male of her choice and then heads off elsewhere to get on
with the business of laying eggs and rearing chicks at her leisure. . . . The male
world, in contrast, is more directly competitive and much less co-operative.
Directly or indirectly, much of its focus lies in mating or in the acquisition of
the resources or status that will create future opportunities for mating.
Advertising becomes a crucial factor in that process.*

Robin Dunbar in *Grooming, Gossip, and the Evolution of Language*

*L*ight as a feather? The feathers of most birds weigh more than their skeleton. How can birds be light enough to fly?

Every aspect of a bird's body is a compromise for life in the air—light enough to fly—but heavy enough to provide high power.

Instead of having sweat glands to lose excess water, birds simply pant, some at a rate of two hundred breaths per minute. Bones, critically needed for strength, are mostly hollow with supporting struts, giving flexibility to withstand the rigors of flight movement without adding weight. Teeth were sacrificed and replaced by gizzards—faster digestion and less cumbersome on the skull, which is filled with the equivalent of a Boeing 747's instrumentation system.

While flight allows birds to get from here to there more efficiently than those of us with feet of clay, birds presumably pay a high cost for it, the flip side of aerobics. Oxygen gives us the fire of life, but it is the oxidization of the body's cells over time that is the aging process.
Jake Page and Eugene S. Morton in *Lords of the Air*

*E*xcept when mating, **hummingbirds** remain solitary. After a showy display to attract attention, males approach females, they mate, then both return to a solitary life.

After the brief mating encounter, females begin nest-building, camouflaging the tiny moss-lined cup with plant down, fibers, and strands of spider silk. The female sits on the pea-sized eggs during incubation and stays with the nest only until the chicks can feed themselves.

Hummingbirds are not monogamous and a percentage are homosexual, both male and female. Several broods per season among hummingbirds are common—females devote close to two weeks for incubation and about three weeks to feeding the chicks, so time is not as available for sex as it is for males.

Anna's Hummingbirds precisely orient the trajectory of their stunning aerial climbs and dives to face into the sun, thereby showing off their iridescent plumage to its best. As a male swoops toward the object of his attentions (either male or female), he resembles a brilliant glowing ember that grows in intensity as he gets closer.

Bruce Bagemihl in *Biological Exuberance*

*H*ummingbirds are known for their high-energy activities. A human heart beats about seventy times per minute—hummingbirds can beat at a steady 1,000 beats per minute. When they fly, they're *flying*—but when they sleep, they don't just sleep, they enter a state of torpor—their heart rate slows to thirty-six beats per minute. After a comatose night, returning to their fast pace is not always possible and many just don't survive the transition. Without a period of slow acclimation, they die.

To expect deep sleepers to wake up fully alert is no less unreasonable than commanding a hummingbird to go from torpor to high-energy activity within a blink. Some humans need to recover from sleep and rarely experience the easy transition from sleep to wakefulness that chipper morning risers show. For many humans, when the connection between the importance of sleep recovery and their daily struggle is acknowledged, the problem is resolved—allowing time for a gradual transition removes the stress.

I rise broken with fatigue each morning.
But the coming of the dawn gives me courage.
Claude Monet

May 6

_____

Human beings are not born once and for all on the day their mothers give birth . . . life obliges them over and over again to give birth to themselves.
Gabriel García Márquez

*H*awk moths, also called sphinx moths, are often mistaken for hummingbirds because of their size and their ability to hover in front of flowers. Nectar feeders like hummingbirds, and almost as big, hawk moths have long, flexible tongues that reach deep into the flowers for the juice. They feed from many of the same flowers that hummingbirds choose.

Night flyers, hawk moths search for white aromatic flowers whose scent they detect with large antennae. During the day they rest on trees, their mottled wings camouflaged neatly against the bark.

The hawk moth shown here (*Manduca quinquemaculata*) matures from a larval stage known as the hornworm, a creature with no resemblance to the moth it becomes. Hornworms pupate in tough leathery cases underground until mature in the spring, when they emerge as night flying moths.

The world has some profound effects on our development, and this fact allows us to remake ourselves through conscious choice, even in adulthood. Yet we can never abandon our inherent natures, our roots.
Robert Ornstein in *The Roots of the Self*

The beauty of the **housefly** (*Musca domestica*) is only surpassed by her offspring. Her eggs look like dark brown grains of rice that miraculously hatch into maggots within one day. Maggots, small legless white worms, are plentiful—females lay five or six batches with more than one hundred eggs in each batch. Shown here is the housefly with eggs and larvae.

Maggots eat dead and decaying animals, cleaning up areas while recycling the animals for the good of all wildlife.

Maggots also heal deep infected wounds—in humans. They eat only dead and dying tissue, *with* the accompanying bacteria—and they leave behind a chemical called *allantoin*, which sterilizes the tissue.

Maggots are superior to antibiotics since they work *only* on the wound. Antibiotics travel through the entire body, killing off good bacteria along the way.

It has long been known among indigenous cultures that when people forget their place in the web of life without periodically renewing connection with the sacred, illness and disharmony follow.
Stephen Harrod Buhner in *Sacred Plant Medicine*

Sometimes he changes his notation so conspicuously that he seems to be improvising sets of variations. It is a meditative, questioning kind of music, and I cannot believe that he is simply saying, "thrush here."

Lewis Thomas in *The Lives of a Cell*

The song of the **wood thrush** (*Hylocichla mustelina*), described as liquid gold, is soft and low-pitched—the longer wavelengths travel around trees and obstacles from the male's ground position so his song will reach his mate. Wavelengths from higher-pitched songs—those of warblers for example—are easily carried across treetops where they typically sing.

Humans can't detect the whole range of notes that birds sing—if the songs of the wood thrush are as extravagant as the poets have been describing for centuries, what must the birds hear? As John Platt says in *The Steps to Man*, "it is enough to make you tingle all the time."

A male wood thrush sings to his mate much longer than other species—continuously from April through July, long after the female is convinced of his worthiness.

I'd like to thank the guy
who wrote the song
that made my baby
fall in love with me . . .
Who put the bomp in the bomp ba bomp ba bomp . . .
"Who Put the Bomp (in the Bomp Ba Bomp Ba Bomp)"
by Barry Mann and Gerry Goffin

There are pieces to every whole; yet each piece is complete. Don't worry about how they will come together. Work joyfully on the piece that's before you. . . .
Melody Beattie in *Journey to the Heart*

As impressive as his love songs are, the male **wood thrush** has no talent or inclination for nest-building. The female builds the nest by herself, to the accompaniment of his music—and she adds as much creative flair to her art as he does to his music. The nests are similar to those of robins, but smaller with more delicate materials. A compact cup contains thin roots, leaves, grasses, bark, and paper mixed into moist soil. Each season, her work surpasses any human art show entry—and each nest is created with *no hands, art supply stores, critics, art classes. . . .*

She shows up for the nest-making by gathering local products—forming a cup of muddy foundation, then adding layers of raw materials until the nest is the size and shape to fit her and her future eggs perfectly. Compared with fast and sloppy constructionists like mourning doves, the wood thrush devotes as much time as she needs to adjust, redo, tweak, and make her nest exactly right for her body.

Finding the perfect pillow combination for yourself is not frivolous if you want to be happy in life.
Sarah Ban Breathnach in *Simple Abundance*

In its perfect pink blossoming, the bloom of the apple tree does not concern itself
with whether a bee will appear. The blossom does its job just by blossoming.
The bee is drawn to do the rest.

Julia Cameron in *Blessings*

Apple trees (*Pyrus malus*) grow over more parts of the Earth than
any other fruit tree. Even though they grow abundantly all over
North America, they aren't actually native trees. Early European
settlers brought apple trees to the States from Europe in the 1600s.

Apple trees are one of the first to bloom in the spring, and
one of the most aromatic, attracting thousands of bees to the pale
pink flowers for the nectar. As the bees fly off, they carry pollen
from that tree to the next tree they visit.

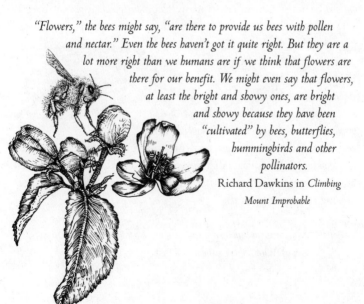

"Flowers," the bees might say, "are there to provide us bees with pollen
and nectar." Even the bees haven't got it quite right. But they are a
lot more right than we humans are if we think that flowers are
there for our benefit. We might even say that flowers,
at least the bright and showy ones, are bright
and showy because they have been
"cultivated" by bees, butterflies,
hummingbirds and other
pollinators.

Richard Dawkins in *Climbing*
Mount Improbable

Up to an inch long, **carpenter ants** (*Camponotus*) are larger than most of the common North American ants. They typically live in dead wood, trees, houses, or under soil, burrowing in chambers made by excavating wood—but not eating it as termites do.

The nests are orderly and well constructed, housing battalions who provide regurgitated food for their queen. Like most ant colonies, workers and soldiers are part of the ant caste but are wingless because they have no need to fly. Males and fertile females who need to leave the nest to mate are the only members with wings.

As in other ant species, carpenters have a complex communication system of chemicals that describe news of the day: "cockroach approaching . . . juicy wounded caterpillar behind rock . . . fire ants closing in from the south."

Ants, like humans, to put it in a nutshell, succeed because they talk so well.
Bert Hölldobler and Edward O. Wilson in *Journey to the Ants*

Whether her lover is Mr. Right or Mr. Right Now, they require romance to feel properly aroused. They are haunted by life, they are a ventriloquist's dummies. Breed, their bodies command, pass on your genes. They gaze into each other's eyes, their mouths open, and they sigh I love you.

Diane Ackerman in *A Natural History of Love*

*L*oving qualities have been attributed to **mourning doves** (*Zenaida macroura*) because of their *lovey-dovey* behavior. Mutual preening, "kissing," pairing off, staying together through nesting—all have the attributes that humans consider a loving nature. Males are constantly heard coo-cooing to attract females during courting.

Mourning doves have more broods than other neighborhood birds—up to six per year. Their nests are loose, almost nonexistent arrangements of a few twigs thrown together as if they couldn't be bothered wasting time with building. They even eat on the run, cramming seeds in a storage area in the throat, called a *crop*, for later digestion.

. . . Love is all a calculated pursuit. Some people spend their lives searching like detectives among all the faces and bodies they can find. . . . But as lovers say, it's not always so easy to know who catches whom, and looking happens in both directions.

James Elkins in *The Object Stares Back*

---

*B*oth male and female **mourning doves** "squeak" when they take off. The squeaks are actually the whistling sounds of their feathers—a distraction to predators. Doves are slow to take off, and the loud, high-pitched noise startles an attacker for one brief moment—long enough to escape.

Mourning doves are as abundant as their extinct cousins were in the 1800s when the U.S. Senate responded to a protective bill with "the passenger pigeon needs no protection."

Their range has been expanding to more northern states, but at a cost: their big, fleshy feet are susceptible to freezing—missing toes are becoming more common among mourning doves in snowy areas.

The dove's song is its most distinctive characteristic. The voice of the dove is the rain song. Out of its mourning, it invokes new waters of life. Its song should remind us that no matter what our life conditions, new waters and new life are still possible. . . . It is a bird of prophecy and can help you to see what you can give birth to in your life.

Ted Andrews in *Animal-Speak*

Some swallowtails mimic other butterflies that are distasteful—benefitting
from their immunity from
predators, even though they
aren't poisonous themselves.
The memory in a bird's brain
of a butterfly with
the same colors
is enough for
them to avoid
the swallowtail.

The deceptive be-
havior of the adult starts during their immature stage
as caterpillars, although the strategy is far different.
The larvae of the **giant swallowtail** (*Papilio cresphontes*) look like
bird droppings on leaves and branches, a close enough camouflage
with crusty white patches on a lumpy brown body, to keep birds
at a distance.

In addition to looking like bird poop, just in case that's not
enough to deter a predator, the swallowtail caterpillar has two
bright orange horns that emit a foul odor when threatened.

The transformation from a smelly blob to a graceful glider is
one of the most miraculous yet commonplace happenings each
spring in backyards, fields, and woods.

The impossible possibility that a man or even a beast might turn into
some wholly different creature seems to fascinate something
buried deep in human nature.
Joseph Wood Krutch in *The Great Chain of Life*

Compared with other butterflies, **swallowtails** are much larger and have long, swallowlike tails extending from the bottom of their wings. These tails might help them glide, but more important, they are used as a protection device.

When a bird attacks a butterfly, it aims for the vulnerable head, with its noticeable antennae—but the "antennae" on the swallowtail are its nonessential wing extensions. The swallowtail can survive with a piece of her wing gone, but not her head.

The butterfly shown here is the zebra swallowtail (*Eurytides marcellus*). Swallowtail wings are primarily orange, red, white, and black. These colors typically warn predators that the butterfly is toxic—or at least disgusting in taste and not worth eating. Some nontoxic female swallowtails imitate the colors of toxic males of another species as a clever way to move freely without being attacked.

Nature gives bounty and variety, but it seldom gives consistency.
Rather, what we can see of nature is full of caprice, trickery, and contradiction
to all of which we respond at least as gratefully as we do to order.
Castle Freeman, Jr., in *Spring Snow*

Rock doves (*Columba livia*), our domestic pigeons, are grain eaters, built to pick up and digest the seeds and grains that fall on tree-lined sidewalks, people-filled parks, fields, backyards, and empty lots. Like the mourning dove, pigeons have a crop to store food at the end of the esophagus, so they can accumulate a lot of seeds at once without having to wait for digestion. When the stomach is ready, the crop releases the stored grain.

Birds have two stomachs, one of which is the gizzard. Gizzards in birds do the grinding that teeth did in prehistoric birds. Why the change? To lighten the load for the airborne animals, birds needed to eliminate the weight in their heads. Teeth were heavy, but without them, the problem of breaking up food remained. Hence the gizzard. The weight was redistributed to a more aerodynamically suitable position.

And what about all those droppings? The laxative effect of plants allows the birds to rapidly discharge the seeds inside fruits. But why would the bird want to drop its load with such haste? It's not the bird, but the seed's tactic to get out before it loses its viability. Five or ten minutes can make the difference between survival and rotting away for a seed. The chemicals in the plants regulate the bird's movements—different time lapses for different birds.

We all consist of the same spirit of creation, although the terms of expression have changed; we now say we contain the same atomic matter as the rest of life, the same DNA as all life-forms.
Linda Hogan in "First People," from *Intimate Nature*

*The ground rule for a territorial species is that individuals that
fail to maintain territory fail to reproduce.*

John Alcock in *Animal Behavior*

Anoles (*Anolis*) are the largest genus of lizards in
the world, with over 250 species. Only the green
anole is native to North America. Anoles are easy
to confuse with chameleons because they change
color so fast, but chameleons are not native to the
United States.

Anoles have long toes with adhesive pads used
to run and climb on smooth surfaces. They can
easily dart away from most predators, but if
caught, they often only lose their tails, which will
eventually regenerate.

After territorial disputes between two
anoles, the winner turns bright green and the
loser brown; hormones in the pituitary glands are
sent through the bloodstream, causing changes in
pigmentation.

The quickest way of ending a war is to lose it.

George Orwell

May 18

*Lacking science, animals seem to have a kind of physical,
or cellular, intelligence that ought to be as miraculous to us as our human
learning might be to them. We have instruments and measurements. They have
senses—many more and better, perhaps, than five. We have logic;
they have repose. We know; they act.*

Castle Freeman, Jr., in *Spring Snow*

$\mathcal{M}$ost striking of all the **anole**'s features is the male's bright throat fan, the *dewlap*. The anole's throat swings forward, displaying a hard-to-ignore yellow, orange, or red flag, used to attract females or to warn trespassers. Typically the male flashes his dewlap while bobbing up and down, the lizard's version of push-ups. What better way to attract a female's attention than by waving a bright red flag through the leaves?

*. . . Visual stimulation from a displaying male does more than simply trigger
the neck-arching response in a receptive female. It actually prepares
recently emerged females to become sexually receptive. . . . Females that are
courted frequently secrete greater quantities of pituitary gonadotropins
than uncourted anoles, speeding ovarian development and the
onset of mating readiness in the spring.*

John Alcock in *Animal Behavior*

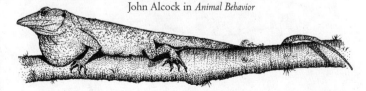

Of all our American salamanders, **tiger salamanders** (*Ambystoma tigrinum*) are the most widespread. They also have the greatest variety of habitats ranging from ponds to moist woods. Black and yellow markings make them easy to identify, although they're not as easily seen as other amphibians such as frogs and toads. When longer daylight hours of spring trigger courtship, salamanders become more visible.

In the spring, males gather at breeding sites, sending messages to females with scents produced by special glands. Females are attracted to these sites and, in turn, use their own scents to convey interest. After dancing around the females for a while, males deposit a jellylike mass of sperm, which his intended will choose if she's sufficiently impressed. She stores his sperm for days, weeks, or sometimes months before using it to fertilize her eggs.

A female's egg is big and filled with protein, fats, nutrients, molecular signals to start the embryo growing; a male's sperm is small and efficiently packaged, nothing more than a serving of genes wrapped in a slippery protein bullet. As the old scientific truism has it, eggs are expensive, sperm is cheap. Small wonder males so often seem willing to blow their pocket change at any opportunity.

Natalie Angier in *The Beauty of the Beastly*

---

*You're neither unnatural, nor abominable, nor mad; you're as much a part of
what people call nature as anyone else; only you're unexplained
as yet you've not got your niche in creation.*
Radclyffe Hall in *The Well of Loneliness*

Similar to frogs, **salamanders** lay their eggs in water. The
eggs develop by undergoing several stages, during which
they move from water to land, the same as frogs—with
one notable oddity not included in the frog's cycle—
some salamanders simply never grow up.
Even as adults, some salamanders
keep their juvenile gills, which allow
them to stay underwater, never leaving the pond where they were born.

*In retrospect, the Native stories are not more far-fetched than the notion
of evolution where fish were transformed into birds, where we people traversed
the same shifting space between species from ape to human.*
Linda Hogan in "First People," from *Intimate Nature*

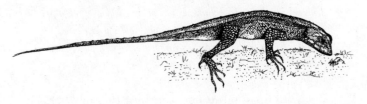

All **lizards,** which are reptiles, have scales, unlike salamanders, which are amphibians and thus smooth-skinned.

The scales on reptiles are similar to the scales on bird legs—and not surprisingly, lizards' skeletons, eyes, and brains are very much the same as those of birds. Both lay eggs and both use an egg tooth to break out of their eggs. Reptiles are cold-blooded, and, at hatching, birds are cold-blooded too—but within days birds become warm-blooded.

Once upon a time there was a lizard with a perfectly good lizard's brain. . . . This simple brain has survived for 200 million years in all animals. . . . The newest and largest addition to the brain is the part that makes us human. The neocortex is rational and lets us store logic, language, mathematics, and speculation about the future. The neocortex lets us consciously change the behavior patterns dictated by our more primitive brains.

Joan Minninger in *Total Recall*

*M*ost lizards have four legs, but **legless lizards** (*Ophisaurus*) have none. Also known as "glass" lizards, their tail is exceptionally fragile and breaks off like glass when threatened. The attacker chases the wriggling tail as the lizard runs to safety, eventually growing a replacement tail.

Much, but no one is sure just how much, of the remainder of the wiring—determining things like whether we get excited about Mozart or baseball; prefer to hike, write sonnets, get in fights, or plant a garden; whether we are rigid, demanding, and stress-prone, or calm, adaptable, and easygoing; whether we tend toward codependency or healthy interdependence— depends on how the basic components of the hardware get wired together by experience. Some of the circuits laid down in the first few years of life are metaphorically cast in stone. They don't change. But some of the wiring remains plastic and reprogrammable, which is why human beings can change, grow, and learn from our experience in ways that our distant ancestors, the lizards, cannot.

Joan Borysenko in *A Woman's Book of Life*

May 23

Great crested flycatchers (*Myiarchus crinitus*) are not great—neither in size nor in crest. Their genus name, *Myiarchus*, is more apt: from the Greek term for "ruler of flies." Flycatchers hunt for insects, catching them on the fly, and will build their nests near wasp- and beehives and orchards where lots of pollinating insects are available.

Loud and aggressive, they defend their nests and territory in aerial combat, often fighting with males of their own kind. A newly mated pair will spend several weeks building their nest—an elaborate creation of twigs, feathers, leaves, and usually at least one snakeskin. When snakeskins aren't available, they insert pieces of cellophane or bubble wrap.

Creating the nest, the flycatcher wanders, flies, pecks, pulls, jams, tugs, loosens, and squishes before the female settles in for egg-laying. This energetic process of "try-this-and-then-try-that" goes on for two weeks or so—noodling around until it's comfortable and protective.

Artists and intellectuals are not the same animal. . . . Younger artists are seedlings. Their early work resembles thicket and underbrush, even weeds. The halls of academia, with their preference for lofty intellectual theorems, do little to support the life of the forest. . . . It took more years and more teaching for me to realize that academia harbors a far more subtle deadly foe to the creative spirit. . . . To be blunt, most academics know how to take something apart, but not how to assemble it.
Julia Cameron in *The Artist's Way*

*I*n the spring and summer **mayflies** (Baetidae) are abundant around streams, rivers, ponds, and lakes. Their lives are short, sometimes not even lasting through a single day. Some species hatch in the evening, and their life cycle is complete and over before dawn. Having no time to eat, many species don't even have stomachs.

To mate, thousands of males dance in huge swarms, encouraging females to enter the mass frenzy. With no time to waste, as soon as a female enters, she mates—and within an hour, she lays her eggs.

Eggs are laid on the water's surface or attached to aquatic plants. When the eggs hatch, a new generation of mayflies swarms above the water, many of which are immediately eaten by fish as they fall back onto the water's surface.

We die from planned obsolescence. Our genetic blueprint comes with a fine print that reads: warranty valid only for a limited time.
Dean Hamer in *Living with Our Genes*

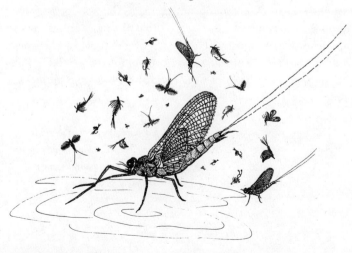

Animals use whatever they can to communicate. **Woodpeckers** (Picidae) bang against trees, telephone poles—any surface that resonates through the neighborhood. The noise attracts attention: of females, of rival males, or to where food can be found.

If humans were to pound their heads against a wall with the same force that woodpeckers use, the brain matter would turn into a pile of mush. The stress is equivalent to a car slamming into a brick wall over and over. But the woodpecker resists the shocks—spongy, protective bone matter absorbs the stress.

Their bodies, too, withstand the intense pressure of pounding, and to hang on, woodpeckers use their strong, clawed feet—two toes pointing front and two back, giving them a viselike grip. They also use their long, stiff tail feathers against the tree to help position and balance themselves.

Pounding into trees also leads to grubs and insects inside the trunk and bark. Once an opening is made, the woodpecker's long tongue reaches far into the narrow hole to extract an insect with the help of sticky material at the tip of the tongue. The woodpecker's head has a storage area to contain the tongue that is literally looped from its bill to the back of its head and all the way around the entire skull.

Although woodpeckers have well-developed voices, they tap or drum in
situations where other birds would call or sing. When they find a metal gutter
or wooden siding on a house, they can hardly resist beating tattoos
so loud that they distress householders who sleep late.
Alexander F. Skutch in *The Minds of Birds*

In the middle of difficulty lies opportunity.
Albert Einstein

The larvae of **antlions** (Myrmeleontidae) are also known as doodlebugs. The mature antlion is a familiar graceful flying insect, but for the first few years of its life, a doodlebug hides in dirt as a dirt-colored, chubby monster with venomous jaws. Unable to fly or run, and too small to defend itself against larger predators, the doodlebug finds safety living in the underworld with no light or food.

By digging and spewing sand from underground, the doodlebug constructs sandpits aboveground with holes through which neighboring animals might slip. The pits look like inside-out anthills. When small insects walk near the rim of the pit, one grain of sand might come loose, creating an avalanche that carries the doomed insect through the opening into the waiting jaws of the doodlebug below.

The drama continues when the doodlebug injects a powerful venom into the insect, paralyzing and liquefying it—ultimately to be sucked dry by the doodlebug. The empty carcasses are tossed from the pit as casually as shrimp and lobster shells are discarded by seafood lovers.

Just remain in the center, watching. And then forget that you are there.
Lao-tzu

. . . When we act in accordance with our truest nature,
we access and express our vein of gold.
Julia Cameron in *The Vein of Gold*

The transformation from underground doodlebug to airborne **antlion** is no less miraculous than Clark Kent leaving a phone booth as Superman.

After living underground for two or three years as a thick-bodied, hairy larva, the doodlebug builds a cocoon in which it pupates—emerging in the warm weather as a graceful thin-bodied flyer with beautiful lacy wings.

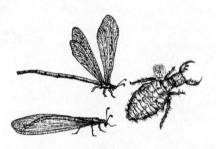

. . . Human beings are actually unfinished animals, constantly in the process of
change and development. At any moment, the maps of our brains may change as
we learn new things and as the world changes. When we learn a new language,
our brain organization changes; if we move to a new city or get married or
divorced, our map changes again. We adapt, we "create ourselves anew"—but
not all of ourselves all the time. For whether we now speak French, have three
kids, or have become the head of the company, we will still dress meticulously or
randomly—maybe Armani random, but still random.
Robert Ornstein in *The Roots of the Self*

Green lacewings (*Chrysopa*) are delicate and pale, usually less than an inch long, with yellow bodies and long, transparent green wings. A common summer insect, lacewings are often seen at night in backyards, fields, gardens, and around doorways and house lights.

Lacewings emerge as winged flying insects after developing inside fuzzy little cocoons attached to leaves. About the size of a rye seed, the larva gathers fibers and hairs, weaving them around its tiny body as an inconspicuous shelter in which to mature. The larvae are also called trashbugs because they attach the shells and skins of nearby dead bugs to their own bodies.

After the immature lacewing emerges from its hairy cocoon, its lumpy brown body has been transformed, along with its aggressive nature, turning out to be a gentle, graceful night flyer with survival tactics far more sophisticated than the brutish monster of its former self.

Can anything happen to you for which you're not ready?
I look back now on certain things that at the time seemed to me to be real
disasters, but the results turned out to be the structuring of a
really great aspect of my life and career.
Joseph Campbell in *An Open Life*

*F*emale **lacewings** lay eggs, one at a time, at the ends of long silk stalks they attach to leaves. This method of egg-laying prevents the larvae from eating each other as they emerge from their eggs. The cannibalistic offspring have sharp jaws and a mean streak as ferocious and aggressive as their parents are gentle and shy.

Immediately after hatching, the larvae reach out their sharp strong jaws to attack and devour anything in their path, including their brothers and sisters. Another common name for these immature lacewings is aphid lion, from their ability to consume massive amounts of aphids.

. . . Leaving aside the deep question as to whether the lower animals have anything going on in their minds that we might accept as conscious thought, are there important events occurring in our human minds that are matched by habits of the animal mind?
Lewis Thomas in *The Fragile Species*

*I*nsect-eating bats commonly dart through summer night skies looking for food, which they snatch on the fly. How do **lacewings,** also looking for food during summer nights, escape the bats' exceptional navigational skills? Lacewings are sensitive to the bats' high-frequency sounds used to locate prey. As a bat flies toward a lacewing, the lacewing detects the approach and plunges toward Earth with folded wings in a power dive that leaves the bat with an empty mouth. This is a great tactic in its own right, but nothing compared to its backup strategy.

The lacewing has another defense: *chaos.* If an attacking bat gets too close for the lacewing to dodge with its power dive, the lacewing performs a wild, crazy, and erratic midair flapping dance—as unpredictable and crazy as possible. In the wake of confusion, the "out-of-control" lacewing escapes, leaving behind a stunned and, once again, empty-mouthed bat.

Lacewings and moths need not have the vaguest mental image of a bat nor any idea of the danger they represent. It is sufficient that they have inherited the neural "wiring" that automatically helps them avoid predators.
John Alcock in *Animal Behavior*

*T*o avoid being fatally attacked by birds, **gray hairstreaks** (*Strymon melinus*) have false antennae at the ends of their wings. These antennae are actually long, thin tendrils growing from the wings, used to deceive predators—as the butterfly feeds, the tendrils are more noticeable than their true antennae and attract a predator's attention. If a bird swoops toward the gray hairstreak to grab a quick meal, it nips the butterfly's wing tips rather than its head—damaging but not fatal.

Looking is looking at or for or just away. Everything that the eye falls on has some momentary interest and possible use. . . . And there is a curious thing here that easily passes unnoticed: I do not focus on anything that is not connected in some way with my own desires and actions. . . . My eyes can understand only desire and possession. Anything else is meaningless and therefore invisible.

James Elkins in *The Object Stares Back*

*A*bundant and common in the summer, **june bugs** (*Phyllophaga*) are clumsy little dive-bombers whose shock-resistant bodies slam into anything in their path. Rambunctious males bounce, crash, and ricochet off doors, lights, human heads, and walls in their relentless urgency to find females.

Females, whose wings are too small to fly well, usually stay in the grass and bushes, assessing the males as they crash to the earth. After crash-landing, the stunned male needs about a minute to reorganize his wings, get his balance, and resume his erratic flight. Through evolution, these relatives of the scarab exchanged flight mobility for hard protective wings.

After mating, eggs are laid in underground nests a few inches below the surface. Within a few weeks the larvae hatch, but they go farther underground for their first few years, coming close to the surface each spring as if deciding if they're ready to emerge. After several years of living underground, they begin their life of flying, mating, and reproducing.

Life is always attempting to move us in the direction of our own evolution and development . . . every experience and event of our lives is part of that process.
Shakti Gawain in *Creating True Prosperity*

$\mathcal{T}$he roots and leaves of **coneflowers** (*Echinacea purpurea*) are commonly sold in pill form to help boost humans' immune system. Native Americans chew the root to relieve toothaches, neck pain, and snake bites.

In addition to its healing capabilities, the wild flowers attract butterflies, bees, and birds to gardens and fields.

Echinacea is used specifically for those who feel shattered by severe trauma in their lives. They may feel profoundly alienated, unable to contact that inner place of strength and calm. Echinacea helps to bring about a sense of wholeness, and greater resilience when under enormous stress . . . for those who lack a sense of identity because of the anonymity of modern life, or who, because of physical or emotional trauma, feel as if they are "falling apart." Such threats to the sense of self may underlie many immune-related illnesses. It strengthens the sense of self and engenders a feeling of wholeness.
Anne McIntyre in *Flower Power*

*Like a good scientist, the transformed self experiments, speculates, invents,
and relishes the unexpected.*
Marilyn Ferguson in *The Aquarian Conspiracy*

*I*n the 1920s and 1930s, you could go into a drugstore and rent a
leech (*Hirudo medicinalis*) for a quarter to
take the black out of a black eye
or the blue out of a black-
and-blue mark. Even though
leeches accomplished these
tasks, sophisticated humans
and modern medicine
turned their rigid
backs on the unap-
preciated leech.
Leeches, however, regained their position in the medical community with recent scientific discoveries: their salivary glands produce a substance called *hirudin* that numbs wounds and stops
clotting. Once it has penetrated the skin, a leech must keep the
blood of its host flowing, so the anticoagulant hirudin in its saliva
takes care of that. Medical professionals now use hirudin to treat
hemorrhoids, rheumatism, thrombosis, and other problems
caused by blood-clotting.

*We are our own raw material. Only when we know what we're made of, and
what we want to make of it, can we begin our lives. . . . To be authentic is,
literally, to be your own author, to discover your own native energies
and desires, and then to find your own way of acting on them.*
Warren Bennis in *On Becoming a Leader*

Today more than 65,000 **leeches** are used each year in hospitals. One of their jobs is to heal severed body parts. Leeches hang on to their host by their rear end while their mouth, a disk-shaped organ, sucks blood. Once it has filled its expandable body, it can live for months. Bacteria in the leeches' gut prevent the blood from decaying.

Although related to worms, leeches can't crawl. Instead, they use their suckers at both ends of their body to loop forward, up and over, like a Slinky moving down stairs.

Leeches can change shape from flat to fat by filling up with blood. Even though they can drink ten times their own weight, the host isn't harmed and doesn't necessarily feel pain from the sucking. When full, the leech drops off and rests.

The biting and blood-sucking action of the leech relieves
the built-up pressure on the tissue until new capillaries can grow and
veins can carry the blood away naturally. . . . Scientists believe
that the leech is a veritable living pharmacy, and that
there are more active chemicals still to be found.
Peggy Thomas in *Medicines from Nature*

Ants use touching and smelling to communicate, constantly giving and receiving news about food, danger, and events crucial for survival of their group.

Two approaching ants communicate by feeling antennae for identification, then by touching mouths, then, if suspicious, they raise their pincers. If one ant determines the other to be a faker, the enlightened ant might yank a body part from the imposter—or simply drag the imposter away to be dealt with by the captor's relatives.

Some ants can fake their way into an unsuspecting colony by disguising themselves with a familiar scent. Once in, the con ants release chemicals to confuse the community, during which the invaders take slaves back to their own group. The tricksters may also take larvae back to their own colony, raised as slaves to work for the good of their community.

> *Ants are so much like human beings as to be an embarrassment.*
> *They farm fungi, raise aphids as livestock, launch armies into wars, use*
> *chemical sprays to alarm and confuse enemies, capture slaves. . . .*
> *They do everything but watch television.*
> Lewis Thomas in *The Lives of a Cell*

Somebody—or if you prefer, Something—didn't know when to stop.
Beetles exist in myriad varieties. Butterflies, a little loftier, make it into high
digits. In our culture, God is so often thought of in terms of Calvinist austerity
and renunciation that we forget there was clearly a godly glee in creative
excess, an artist in love with the materials themselves.
Julia Cameron in *The Vein of Gold*

Scientists estimate that 95 percent of the species on the planet are insects—and one in every four animals is a **beetle**—a humbling array of almost half a million species, each with a creativity that most artists only dream about.

Beetles are fanciful, colorful, bizarre, gemlike, serious, playful—and as action characters, they surpass all video game strategists. Looking at the details of any beetle, you can almost hear the creator's glee: "Yes, that's it, another dot over here, and a little stroke over here, stick some horns on top and some emeralds underneath . . . now let's add some rhinestones, fake fur, and daggers. . . ."

Let our minds play with ideas; let our senses gather information; and let the rich
interaction proceed as it must (for the mind processes what the senses gather,
while a disembodied brain, devoid of all external input, would
be a sorry instrument indeed).
Stephen Jay Gould in *Dinosaur in a Haystack*

*B*utterflies visit red and white flowers less often than they do other colors. But some butterflies, like the **gulf fritillary** (*Agraulis vanillae*), are attracted to both. Their own colors are flashy and metallic, and typical of most butterflies, the underwing patterns are extremely different from the outerwing. This allows for better camouflage when their wings are folded and better attraction when open.

Fritillaries energetically fly from flower to flower testing and tasting, avoiding poisonous plants, and dodging predators. For all their delicate beauty, butterflies are tough, wary, and resilient.

> *To the Native Americans, the butterfly is a symbol of change, joy, and color.*
> *The colors of the butterfly should be examined for its significance and*
> *to help you understand the role within your life. . . . Butterfly*
> *medicine reminds us to make changes when the*
> *opportunities present themselves.*
> Ted Andrews in *Animal-Speak*

One of the common irritants to humans in the summer is the **chigger,** which is simply a harvest mite (*Trombicula*) before it becomes an adult. Even though much smaller than ticks, these chigger larvae can bite with more intensity, causing painful itching and hundreds of tiny welts.

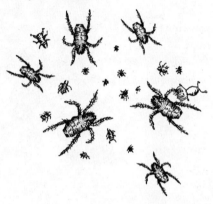

When chiggers hatch from their eggs, they immediately look for fresh blood. When they find a host, often a human, they clamp on to a hair follicle or a skin pore. There they inject a digestive juice that disintegrates skin cells, which they eat. The skin area becomes red and swollen, sometimes enveloping the chigger, giving the false impression that the tiny creature has burrowed under the skin. Even after the chigger is killed, the itching continues for a few days.

. . . If we had keen vision and a feeling for all ordinary human life, it would be like hearing the grass grow and the squirrel's heart beat, and we should die of the roar which lies on the other side of silence.

George Eliot

Ants, living in a colony, function as a single mind to take care of cleaning, building, defending, hunting, teaching, and informing.

Dr. Lewis Thomas calls them "tiny, genetic machines with no options for behavior ... generation after mindless generation."

But are they so mindless? Moving as one unit, some ant species are able to conquer formidable and huge insects, a live moth or bee, by calling for recruits or heading back to the nest to ask for help—but not without leaving a telltale trail pointing the way to the cargo. Any related ant within smelling distance of the trail cooperates by joining forces, driven to a mission for the highest good of the colony.

> *In our view, the competitive edge that led to the rise of the ants as a world-dominant group is their highly developed, self-sacrificial colonial existence. It would appear that socialism really works under some circumstances. Karl Marx just had the wrong species.*
> Bert Hölldobler and Edward O. Wilson in *Journey to the Ants*

---

*A*mong female **beetles,** emitting sex pheromones to attract males is common—but why would male beetles emit *female* sex pheromones, as they are known to do? Researcher Klaus Peschke studied some beetles thriving on a maggot-rich rotting carcass. Both sexes coexisted until females started wandering away to lay eggs, leaving behind a predominantly male population.

The few females who remained in the carcass were protected from the males' aggressive behavior by their chemical smell. If young males could imitate the female odor, they might stand a chance to survive the onslaught of the stronger, older males. And so they did—camouflaging themselves with a convincing smell—convincing enough to fool the older males, *and* attract them to approach the nice-smelling young males with ardor.

The young males ignored the advances of the elders, continuing to eat the plentiful maggots within the carcass. By the time their protective perfume wore off, the young beetles had grown large enough to defend themselves.

Males do the fighting in every society. This is not only because of their greater physical strength but also because it again acts to ensure the survival of the next generation.
Robert Ornstein in *The Roots of the Self*

Some **ants** are solitary wanderers, important members of the colony, as they collect food and information to carry back to the community.

Some ants form teams of two or more to help manage large chunks of food. If a team encounters a situation too big to handle alone, they return to the nest, ask for recruits, and lead the way to the situation.

To communicate all this, a female might raise her abdomen and extend her stinger, which releases a particular chemical signal. Another worker will approach, touch, assess with her antennae, and follow her sister to the place described. Two ants running side by side are probably on yet another mission to help their group.

Humans speak lovingly of extended families, but to an ant the whole society is close kin, and it will die rather than allow its genetic line to dry up. Humans, on the other hand, are related in very small, nuclear families which are in glaring competition with one another. Unlike the ants, we must abolish our self-interest to work together, and that's asking a great deal. It makes altruism all the more remarkable.

Diane Ackerman in *A Natural History of Love*

Human males are roused to lust by pictures in a magazine.
A picture is just printing ink on paper. It is two-dimensional, not three.
The image is only a few inches high....
Richard Dawkins in *River Out of Eden*

$\mathcal{A}$ male wasp is often attracted to an **orchid** because of its resemblance to a female wasp. He approaches the orchid and tries to mate with it, but flies away without the benefit of mating. However, in the process, he collects pollen and carries it to the next flower, giving the orchid a chance to reproduce. The orchid's mimicry—pretending to be something it isn't, simply to get what it wants—is common throughout nature. But how could a wasp be so easily tricked? After all, the orchid is *just* a flower, not an insect.

They are the P. T. Barnums of the flower kingdom, dedicated to the premise that there is a sucker born every minute: a sucker, that is, with wings and thorax, and an unquenchable thirst for nectar and love. They are the orchids, flowers so flashy of hue and fleshy of petal that they seem thoroughly decadent. And when it comes to their wiles for deceiving and sexually seducing insect pollinators, their decadence would indeed make Oscar Wilde wilt.
Natalie Angier in *The Beauty of the Beastly*

When we think of it, there is something truly remarkable in the fact that practically all human beings want to be better than they are. What a hopeful reading of the human race—four billion people, all eager to improve themselves!
Karen Casey and Martha Vanceburg in *The Promise of a New Day*

Fire ants clamp on to flesh with their jaws and then inject venom with their rear-end stingers. Humans usually are bitten by more than one fire ant because the first biter emits an alarm signal to her nest-mates. The mass cooperation among fire ant colony members is efficient and complex. To draw large numbers of helpers to ants in need, a couple of fire ants can re-cruit, within minutes, a swarm of thousands of colony mates.

In the 1930s, a South American fire ant (*Solenopsis invicta*) arrived in Mobile, Ala-bama. Within forty years it had become the dominant ant through the southern United States. During this invasion, the previously dominant fire ant (*S. geminata*) retreated to a smaller range. Their flexibility allowed them to survive in whatever space was available.

There's an awful lot of irrationality in the attitude toward, and hatred of, fire ants. It's just another creature trying to make a living.
Walter Tschinkel, entomologist at Florida State University

Passionflowers (*Passiflora incarnata*) grow wild on vines in woods and roadsides in the southeastern United States.

All parts of this plant are used for food and medicine—tea made from the whole plant helps headaches, tension, stomach pain, and reduces high blood pressure. The egg-shaped fruit is eaten by birds and mammals, including humans.

The passionflower vine is used by certain butterflies such as zebra longwings as the host plant to lay their eggs. When the larvae emerge from the eggs, they begin eating the plant itself. But for its own defense, the plant has a strategy to deter the voracious eaters. Two glands in the plant secrete a sweet liquid to attract ants. Ants are the zebra longwing's greatest enemy, so as long as the plant provides an inducement for the ants, it maintains its own survival.

If we accept that the biology of a species includes its typical behavior and adaptability, then human biology has everything to do with environment: not only has it been shaped by past environments, it also determines how we respond to current environments.

Frans de Waal in *Good Natured*

We will discover the true nature of our particular genius when we stop trying to conform to ours or to other peoples' models, learn to be ourselves, and allow our natural channel to open.
Shakti Gawain

Most **longwings** (Heliconiinae) have such a foul taste that birds stay away from them. This taste comes from toxins in the nectar they eat in passionflower vines. Other insects are repelled by the plant, but the longwings are immune to it, and simply use the toxic chemicals for their own defense.

Immature longwings look nothing like their parents—they have sharp spikes and polka dots on their caterpillar bodies, instead of the graceful striped wings of their parents. But they go through a metamorphosis, like all butterflies, during which they change from chubby crawlers to beautiful aerial gliders.

To be looking elsewhere for miracles is to me a sure sign of ignorance that everything is miraculous.
Abraham Maslow

*A*phids (Aphididae) have soft, pear-shaped, tiny bodies, usually less than one-eighth inch long, with mouths that can suck the juices of a plant dry. They cling to the undersides of leaves and walk vertically on stems by using claws on their feet and sponge-like pads that form a suction when wet.

Billions of aphids and their eggs are eaten by lady beetles, lacewings, and syrphid flies through the spring and summer. The aphids defend themselves and their territory by squirting a gluelike substance from *cornicles,* two tubes sticking from behind like exhaust pipes on a car. The glue fouls up the attacker's ability to walk or fly.

Females also fight for possession of a particular leaf. But why bother when hundreds of leaves are available? Just as in human real estate, some leaves are in better neighborhoods; water, nutrition, shelter, and good protection from danger are some factors that make property valuable. The owner's offspring then have all the advantages of growing up in a healthy neighborhood.

We can live with the same interests as animals: clinging to life, begetting future generations, and winning our place in the world. But then there can open the sense of the spiritual quest and realization—the birth of the spiritual life.
Joseph Campbell in *An Open Life*

*F*emale **aphids** can reproduce without fertilization. Shown here is a female giving birth to a live clone of herself. All the offspring from this birth are identical, of course—and all wingless females. But females can (and do) mate with males to produce offspring of their own. But how do they find males if all offspring are female?

A dozen or more generations of females can be produced solely by a female until over-crowding on a plant or other factors create a response to reproduce sexually. The next cycle will then include males *and* females with wings—and both will leave their host plant and mother to start a new colony.

In one of those idle calculations made from time to time, the eighteenth-century French natural historian René-Antoine Ferchault de Réaumur once figured that any single fertile female aphid could, if unchecked, produce 5 million offspring in its reproductive lifetime of four to six weeks. Hence, for the comfort of all the rest of us animals who inhabit the planet, it is reassuring to have lacewings, ladybugs, and syrphid-fly larvae around to keep this from happening.

Sue Hubbell in *Broadsides from the Other Orders*

June 18

Without ladybugs and some equally staunch allies, the insect Mafia would gain the upper hand and require greater use of chemical pesticides.
Kenneth S. Hagan in "Following the Ladybug Home,"
National Geographic, April 1970

*O*f the hundreds of species of **lady beetles** in the United States, the one shown here (*Hippodamia convergens*) is one of the most abundant and one of the most popular—each lady beetle, during the peak of summer gardening, can consume thousands of aphids and mealy bugs.

After the summer, some lady beetle species migrate to find areas with warmer temperatures; but some move into homes and stay dormant through the winter, hidden in closets and unused spots. When they emerge in the spring, they show up on windowsills and are safely let out to ensure their homes aren't on fire.

The truth is that people like ladybugs, and there are few insects that they do. Ladybugs look as if they were designed by a children's-book author, and they make us smile.
Sue Hubbell in *Broadsides from the Other Orders*

June 19

A healthy **lady beetle** lays clusters of ten to fifty oblong yellow eggs every day for a month or more. Warty-looking larvae, with none of the popular appeal of the parents, emerge from their eggs ready to devour aphids. If aphids aren't available, they simply eat one another. After consuming thousands of aphids, the larvae pupate in yellowish cases attached to plants, before emerging as mature insects. The lady bug of nursery rhyme fame must now find food elsewhere since her former self ate all the available aphids:

> Lady bird, lady bird! Fly away home!
> Your house is on fire,
> Your children do roam,
> Except little Nan, who sits in a pan
> Weaving gold laces
> As fast as she can

*The ladybird, of course, has no home and never did have one. The "children"
do roam, however—in search of aphids and scale insects. All, that is,
except little "Nan." She, alas, cannot "roam" because she is the yellow pupa
and is securely tied to the plant by the handle of the "pan."*
Richard Headstrom in *Nature in Miniature*

A weed is just a plant out of place.
John C. Gifford in *The Reclamation of the Everglades with Trees*

Black-eyed Susans (*Rudbeckia hirta*) grow abundantly throughout the United States in fields, roadsides, and waste areas—available to anyone who notices their big, daisylike yellow flowers among the other weeds and wildflowers.

Native Americans used black-eyed Susans for many remedies, including brewing tea from the roots for colds, and squeezing the root juice for earaches.

I believe that Gaia, mother Earth, is purposeful and that the long-established behavior patterns of indigenous peoples indicated a knowledge of this fact. They developed specific patterns of communication and relationship with other forces larger than themselves. These forces, which they called mother Earth and Creator, we now call Gaia and God.
Stephen Harrod Buhner in *Sacred Plant Medicine*

June 21

Lyme disease is caused by a microscopic, spirally coiled bacterium called *Borrelia burgdorferi*. This organism is spread by an infected tick, *Ixodes dammini*, in the eastern United States and by *Ixodes pacifica* in the western United States. Because these ticks are commonly found on the white-tailed deer, they have become known as deer ticks, but mice, birds, dogs, squirrels, and several other mammals, including humans, are used as hosts. Lyme disease got its name from Olde Lyme, Connecticut, where the first recognized outbreak occurred around 1975.

The ticks, only the size of pepper flakes, are much smaller than the familiar dog tick, and hence much more difficult to spot on a body. If an infected tick stays attached to a human for several hours, the Borrelia organism can enter the body and begin to multiply, spreading through the blood system and ultimately into tissues. The effects of their invasion show up in several ways ranging from flu-like symptoms to loss of muscle control, and can suddenly disappear or reoccur several years later.

Host animals such as deer and mice aren't affected by Lyme disease—only humans and domestic animals.

Would the question of "right and wrong" exist if humans were not on earth? It is hard to believe that animals weigh their own interests against the rights of others, that they develop a vision of the greater good of society, or that they feel lifelong guilt about something they should not have done.

Frans de Waal in *Good Natured*

Pickerelweed (*Pontederia cordata*) is a tall, majestic water plant common in ponds, swamps, streams, and marshes. From summer through fall, large lavender flowers bloom on top of stalks growing out of the water.

Most of this plant is edible, including stems, leaves, and seeds. Seeds are eaten raw, cooked like cereal, or ground into flour for baking.

In our quest for the scientific and rational, we have come to look at nature and its elements as objects separate from us and simply to be studied. For many, this scientific approach to nature has destroyed the mysticism and spirituality surrounding it. . . . Nothing could be further from the truth. What science uncovers about nature should amaze us and fill us with even greater wonder at the magnificent expression of life in all its varied forms.

Ted Andrews in *Animal-Speak*

What we call results are beginnings.
Ralph Waldo Emerson

Some plants, like grasses, use the wind for pollination; some plants use flamboyant blooms to attract bats; some display red tubular flowers to get hummingbirds' attention; and some rely on fragrance at night to attract night moths. Some orchids, such as this **lady's slipper** (*Cypripedium*) look and smell like female insects.

Although no nectar is in its pouch, this orchid lures bees with a nectarlike scent. When the bee is inside the flower, unsatisfied, its only escape is through a narrow channel where its back is coated with pollen—to be dropped off at the next lady's slipper.

. . . There must be some substantial benefits to playing sexual roulette, otherwise natural selection wouldn't permit it to be such a driving obsession amongst almost all of animal and plant life.
Richard Dawkins in *Climbing Mount Improbable*

*To err is human, we say, but we don't like the idea much, and it is
harder still to accept the fact that erring is biological as well. We prefer sticking
to the point, and insuring ourselves against change. But there it is:
we are here by the purest chance, and by mistake at that.*

Lewis Thomas in *The Medusa and the Snail*

The pods of the **milkweed** (*Asclepias*)
contain hairy seeds that drift in the air.
With millions of milkweed plants and insect
pollinators active day and night
for several months, why isn't the
earth overrun by milkweeds? The
pollination process of an insect
carrying baggage from one
flower to another is not as productive as it
may seem. For one thing, if an insect inserts
a load of pollen backward, the pollen grains germinate in the
wrong direction—and are wasted.

*A plant, a fixed rooted thing,
immobilized in a single spot, had
devised a way of propelling its offspring
across open space. Immediately there passed
before my eyes the million airy troopers of the
milkweed pod . . . yet the ability to do this
had not been with them at the beginning.
It was the product of endless effort
and experiment.*

Loren Eiseley in *How Flowers Changed the World*

Water fleas (*Daphnia pulex*) are microscopic creatures living in ponds, ditches, and wherever still water is found. They move through the water with erratic jump starts by jerking their antennae.

Their reproduction abilities would make headlines if they were larger, more familiar animals. Water fleas are ready to reproduce when only a week or so old, producing fertile eggs without a partner. Their eggs, seen clearly through transparent bodies, as shown here, produce all females. Then these females (which are all duplicates of their mother) begin reproducing within a week, still with no mates. This continues for many generations until, as if by some unseen signal, water fleas begin giving birth to females *and* males.

This new generation mates, but their offspring are different from past generations—these eggs drop to the bottom of the pond and lie dormant until something triggers them to hatch, typically when air temperature and moisture turn favorable. This can happen the following spring or even a few years later.

I am part of the natural world. As part of it, I have a responsibility to know as much about the environment in which I am living. The more I understand it, the more I understand myself.

Ted Andrews in *Animal-Speak*

What's the difference between **frogs** and **toads**? Both are cold-blooded, nocturnal, and have similar shapes and behaviors. Their differences are often hazy, but generally, toads (*Bufo*) have warty skin and short legs that they use to hop short distances—hence, their nickname "hoptoads." Frogs (*Rana*) however, have long, strong legs, which allow them to jump fast and far, leaping out of danger and traveling farther than toads—hence their nickname "leapfrog." But, typical of nature, exceptions are always present.

Males, both toads and frogs, use their voices to attract females. Each species has a distinctive call, recognized by the females of the same species.

. . . Human males have been under intense selection pressure to evolve deeper voices during their sexually active years. They have to compete with each other for access to females for mating, and yelling matches have been (and still are) part of the process whereby rivalries are settled. Females have no need to develop deep voices because they do not compete with men or with each other in quite the same way.

Robin Dunbar in *Grooming, Gossip, and the Evolution of Language*

During the summer **American toads** (*Bufo americanus*) are found around almost any moist habitat in the United States—backyards, woods, streams, ditches. Distinctive features are the large, puffy bumps behind their eyes, *paratoid* glands, which are filled with poison (and which probably gave toads the false reputation of causing warts). When dogs or cats bite into a toad, the poison is released, making the animal sick, sometimes fatally, or at least with a foul taste in its mouth.. Nevertheless, some pets continue to bite toads throughout the summer.

Toads, on the other hand, learn from their mistakes if they eat something toxic such as a millipede, which has a nauseatingly bad taste. As soon as they bite into it, they spit it out and never eat one again. The toad "learns" from this one bad experience, instead of "knowing" instinctively as in some other animals—garter snakes "know" from birth to avoid poisonous food. Does "learned" behavior shift to "instinctual" behavior after several successful generations?

Sometimes it's easy to forget that our brains evolved to solve such basic Stone Age problems as courting a mate, finding food, making kinship bonds, devising a language, cooperating with other members of the tribe, sharing food, braving the environment, and fighting to keep oneself and one's offspring alive. Problems vital to our survival.

Diane Ackerman in *A Slender Thread*

The coloring and designs of **garter snakes** (*Thamnophis*) vary, but almost all have three yellowish stripes running the length of their bodies.

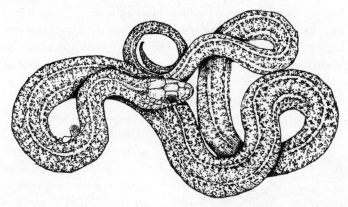

Behavior among garters also varies among different species. During mating, some males "seal in" sperm with a gel-like plug to keep other males from getting their sperm into a female; the smell alone is enough to deter competing males. However, not all males want to compete. It is common among some animals to change sex as they mature, and for some animals to acquire opposite-sex characteristics. "Some male Common Garter Snakes for example, produce a scent that resembles the female pheromone, causing males to mistake them for females and attempt to court and mate with them," according to Bruce Bagemihl in *Biological Exuberance.*

People are both repelled and fascinated by snakes, even when they have never seen one in nature. . . . Manhattanites dream of them with the same frequency as Zulus.
Edward O. Wilson in *The Diversity of Life*

Frogs and toads are characterized by their "pop-eyes." These bulging eyes help them swallow by pushing food down into the throat when they close their eyes.

Each night hundreds of insects are caught and pulled into their mouths with their long, flypaperlike tongues. With all the abundant food, do they ever stop eating? Yes, frogs have nerve cells that signal available food—a nearby worm, for example—and they respond by eating the worm. When their biological needs change, a cue from the nerve cells adjusts their response, and they stop responding to the "eat the worm" signal.

When humans continue eating even after we're "full," is it because our signals have failed? Or because we don't know how to read the signals? Or because we ate too fast, not giving the signals time to work? Or is it because the detectors are still waiting to be satisfied—an impossibility with food that contains no primal "satisfaction ingredients"?

> ... *The average American today has a choice of 50,000 different food products in the supermarket compared with about 500 products at the turn of the century, and the average American today expends only about one-fourth the calories of an average American in 1900.... While our ancestors also were obsessed with food—finding it, that is—our obsession is more refined.... We have separated food from hunger at a time when the supply is unlimited.*
> Dean Hamer in *Living with Our Genes*

Bullfrogs (*Rana catesbeiana*) are the largest of our North American frogs and one of the most visible. Their smooth green, yellow, and brown bodies are familiar around lakes, ponds, bogs, and streams in the summer. They are mostly solitary, but males interact with other males, usually in confrontations, in the spring.

But where do the frogs go in the winter? A bullfrog, to protect itself from the cold, burrows down into the soft mud on the bottom of still water and remains motionless through the winter. Since it needs little oxygen to breathe in this dormant state, it takes in, through its skin, what's available from the moisture in the mud. In the spring, it returns to the surface, using its back feet like flippers to push upward.

With the first warm spring evenings, bullfrog croaks are heard mingling with the chirps of night insects. Their bass voices continue through the summer as males and females search for the right mate.

I have always liked frogs. I liked them before I ever took up zoology as a profession; and nothing I have ever had to learn about them since has marred the attachment. I like the looks of frogs, and their outlook, and especially the way they get together in wet places on warm nights and sing about sex.
The music frogs make at night is a pleasant thing, full of optimism and inner meaning. . . .
Archie Carr in *The Windward Road*

A familiar sound in spring and summer, the deep voices of male **bullfrogs** are heard from grassy habitats or from the surface of a pond where they may be floating on vegetation. Bullfrogs have an internal vocal sac so their throats don't swell like the other male frogs; however, their voices are strong and far-reaching— as "jug-a-rum, jug-a-rum" is repeated over and over to attract females. From the loud chorus some eventually drop out, exhausted from using up too much oxygen to sing. Females notice which males last through the night— she won't waste her time with a mate who can't hold a tune and thus probably won't provide the best sperm available.

In addition to having to sing well, males also have to choose the best possible territory as a way to attract females; good shelter and food supplies are necessary for healthy egg development, a big concern for his future mate. A female is first drawn to an area by the songsters, but then she'll choose the largest male around since he'll be the one who can defeat smaller males and defend her prime real estate. The best nursery grounds produce the healthiest tadpoles.

A far more common way for females to get resources from their mate is to go to a territory controlled by a male and to exchange a copulation in return for access to the goods within the area.
John Alcock in *Animal Behavior*

*C*ricket frogs (*Acris*) live in grasses and reeds at the edges of ponds and streams. Even though cricket frogs are more active during the day than other frogs, males still rely on the night to send out their trill chorus to attract mates.

Like most other frogs, cricket frogs have visible eardrums behind their eyes that are sensitive to vibrations, giving them excellent hearing.

All that loud croaking and competing for a female frog on summer nights has more complexity to it than what meets the ear. For one thing, even though each frog would like to be the loudest, biggest, and most attention-getting male on the bog, he must be careful not to get *too* much attention or his predators will know where to find the plumpest and tastiest frog.

> *Resorting to deep-bellied sounds is almost universal across human cultures in situations where we want to create a lasting impression. . . . Successful public speakers do not squeak and warble in falsetto, but lower the pitch of their voice.*
> Robin Dunbar in *Grooming, Gossip, and the Evolution of Language*

Millions of frog eggs hatch during warm weather, changing from legless embryos with tails to mature frogs with limbs and lungs with less of a to-do than Jacques Cousteau slipping out of dive gear.

A **tadpole** is the transition stage of a frog before it develops legs. The transformation from an egg to a frog occurs as routinely among amphibians as hopping from one lily pad to another—unremarkable except that changing from a water animal to a land creature is no less miraculous than if humans developed gills to breathe underwater.

Of the millions of eggs that become tadpoles each summer, only a few will reach maturity—and of those that do become frogs, only a few will survive. Attack by predators at all stages explains the phenomenal numbers born each year.

Frog spawn coats a moonlit pond only briefly before most of it is devoured by predators. If but a few eggs survive to become tadpoles, and a few tadpoles become frogs, everything is working right. . . . humans give birth to very few young, only one a year in most cases. If that child dies, there are no backups.
Diane Ackerman in *A Natural History of Love*

July 4

$\mathcal{F}$ireflies (Lampyridae) use chemically created flashes to get sex or food—the two major concerns of insects—or as a way to get sex *for* food.

Their flashes are a series of dots and dashes—a firefly's Morse code. Color and brightness are added for emphasis. The signals are the male's calling card, advertising who he is. A female, in turn, flashes back, letting him know she's receptive. Simple enough—and this system has worked for generations, but, as is nature's way, other fireflies have found a way to work the system for their own purposes.

Spiders are the main enemy of fireflies, but, with a certain toxin, most fireflies will be left alone. To become "immune," a firefly must eat another firefly with the toxins. To attract the species with these chemicals, females intercept those males while in pursuit of their own females. In response to his flash, the devious female will fake her interest by imitating the flash of *his* species. When the male sees the female answering with the correct signal, he approaches her—but meets with his murderer rather than his lover. She eats him and thus receives his protective chemicals.

However, not to be outdone by these shifty females, a male firefly of *her own* species takes advantage of her sneakiness by pretending to be her potential dinner—but when she arrives, he blinks his true identity and mates with her.

The truth dazzles gradually, or else the world would be blind.
Emily Dickinson

July 5

Leopard frogs (*Rana pipiens* and *R. sphenocephala*) are one of the most widely distributed amphibians in the United States. Green and brown spots on either side of light ridges running down their backs camouflage them well in the vegetation of marshes, ponds, streams, and woods.

During mating season, the colors of many frogs change. Pigment cells under their transparent skin deepen or brighten to get the attention of the opposite sex. The level of melatonin, a hormone that affects skin pigmentation, drops as daylight hours increase in the spring. Sex organs function again after a winter of darkness when melatonin levels were high. Biological urges originating in the pineal glands in humans are often light-driven and correspond with melatonin levels. Who knows how much human behavior is determined by seasonal light when ancient urges are triggered by more or less light?

. . . A curious thing about these frogs is that they stray so far from water, much farther than most other frogs, which are practically aquatic animals. Maybe the leopard frog represents the advance guard of frog evolution, separating itself from water more than its cousins, preparing for a fully terrestrial life.

Castle Freeman, Jr., in *Spring Snow*

*B*agworms (Psychidae) build homes around themselves from available sticks, leaves, fibers, and twigs. They dangle from their host plant like little Chinese lanterns, many dozens hanging camouflaged through the year. Inside each case is a silky sack in which the wingless female moths spend their entire lives. Males have wings but typically only leave their structures to mate.

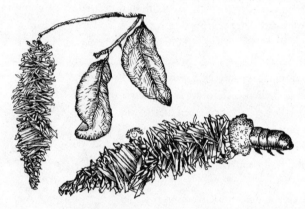

In the northeast United States, the small bagworms use evergreen needles to construct homes. In the south, each species uses a particular plant's leaves and stems. The bagworm shown here (*Thyridopteryx ephemeraeformis*), from the south, builds from leaves and stem pieces from the ixora plant.

Bagworms have no wings, eyes, legs, or antennae, and they never leave their bags, even laying their eggs inside.

We are all intended to create. It's in our spiritual DNA.
Julia Cameron in *The Vein of Gold*

July 7

For many people—most people really—change is possible, even necessary....
Even seemingly miraculous transformations of the self may occur.
We won't know unless we try.

Laurence Miller in *Inner Natures*

Caddisflies (Phryganeidae) are mothlike insects related to butterflies, but instead of scales on their wings they have hairs. The
name of their order, Trichoptera, means "hairy wings." Evidently,
during evolution, the original hairy wings of butterflies and
moths changed to scales, but the wings of caddis insects remained
hairy.

Over 1,000 species of caddisflies live in North America.
Adults are commonly seen flying around house lights in the summer, until the females leave to lay their masses of eggs in nearby
streams and ponds.

Their eggs hatch within a few days and
the larvae begin to build protective cases
around themselves from scraps of nearby material underwater, where they will live while developing. The looks and
lifestyles of the young underwater
caddis insects are mysteriously unlike their airborne parents.

Be patient. You'll know when it's time for you to wake up and move ahead.

Baba Ram Dass

Caddisfly larvae are the bagworms of the water. But unlike bagworms, who stay in their protective cases on land their entire lives and never change form, caddisworms undergo complete metamorphosis, leaving the water after about a year to emerge as mothlike insects with fully developed wings.

The term *caddis* came from "caseflies"—each larva builds a case around itself in which it lives while becoming a mature insect. The cases are made from stones, leaves, twigs, sand, fibers, and any other available marine debris. The larvae have sharp jaws to cut through tough leaves, bark, and grass. Small stones, shells, and discarded pieces are glued on as an artistic flourish.

Each species creates its own distinctive case, usually with a style that identifies the artist. One of the most creative is a miniature net built by one species, to collect particles of food drifting in the water, similar to the seines used by humans to catch seafood.

Each of us has a genius within us waiting to be released.
Henry David Thoreau

Hundreds of species of **dragonflies** live around ponds, streams, marshes, and lakes throughout North America. The regal darner (*Coryphaeschna ingens*), shown here, has lacy wings, a long thin body, and big head—typical of all dragonflies. The head is hollow in the back so it can rotate, not only sideways, but up, down, and diagonally, giving it that peculiar and curious stare seen so often in dragonflies.

Eggs are laid in water and hatch into thick-bodied insects that have little resemblance to their parents or to the graceful flyers they eventually become. Powerful jaws of the nymphs extend at, attack, and grab mosquito larvae, which they pull into their mouths with lightning speed.

Their development in water lasts up to several years. They molt several times, then emerge from the water as graceful aerial acrobats. Their ability to catch and eat millions of mosquitoes in midflight gives them their common name, mosquito hawks.

> . . . *Call on Dragonfly to guide you through the mists of illusion to the pathway of transformation. See how you can apply the art of illusion to your present question or situation, and remember that all things are never completely as they seem.*
> Jamie Sams and David Carson in *Medicine Cards*

What's the difference between a **dragonfly** and a **damselfly**? The most visible difference is that the dragonfly's wings are always open, even when perching. A damselfly perches with its wings closed over its back. Dragonflies are much more powerful fliers than damselflies, but both are able to dodge and maneuver with an agility that helicopter designers would like to imitate.

Their body structure is remarkably efficient and agile—it hasn't changed for the last 300 million years.

The ancestors of insects were creatures of the sea—and some, like dragonflies and damselflies, have reentered the water, spending most of their lives underwater to emerge, relatively short-lived, out of water. Some of the water dwellers live for years in water as they transform into adults whose lives may last only a few weeks.

Whether they belong to more evolved species like humans, or simpler ones such as animals, all beings primarily seek peace, comfort, and security.
Life is as dear to a mute animal as it is to any human being;
even the simplest insect strives for protection from dangers that threaten its life.
Tenzin Gyatso, fourteenth Dalai Lama, in *A Human Approach to World Peace*

*Securing copulations is a major ultimate goal of male behavior in most species;
but as [this] damselfly illustrates, copulation itself is no guarantee
that a male will fertilize his mate's eggs.*
John Alcock in *Animal Behavior*

After a conspicuous courtship display of spreading his wings and lifting his abdomen, the male **damselfly** leads the female to his territory. He then lands on her back, grasping her with special claspers, and loops his abdomen toward her so he can transfer his sperm into her. He holds on to her long enough to be sure his sperm is safely inside before releasing her. Then, however, he stays near her to guard his investment, even during the egg-laying process. If he doesn't guard her, he risks losing his investment. . . .

To deposit eggs, the female perches on a floating plant and releases her eggs into the water. If she is unguarded and another male happens to fly by, the new male has an opportunity to continue *his* line of genes—he scoops out the previous male's sperm with a special organ and inserts his own sperm.

*Johnny get angry, Johnny get mad,
Gimme the biggest lecture I ever had.
I wanna brave man, I wanna caveman.
Johnny show me that you care, really care for me.*
"Johnny Get Angry" by Hal David and Sherman Edwards

July 12

Male **dragonflies** are highly territorial, defending their area by attacking intruding dragonflies in midair clashes. The loser usually drowns after an aerial blast.

Their short life as adults, lasting only a few weeks, is occupied with defending territory, finding partners, and ultimately mating and laying eggs. With so much to accomplish in so short a time, the intensity increases, as does the competition.

By necessity, females are much choosier than males about selecting mates. A female's investment in time and energy is much greater than his, and males can impregnate more females in a shorter time and are available for sex throughout their lifetime, while the female is dedicated to one clutch of eggs. Competition for sex is often seen with thousands of dragonflies paired in loops near waterways during the hottest weeks of the summer.

Entomologists fall into two categories: those who find insects endlessly fascinating and those who would get rid of them. . . . Those who would get rid of insects are afflicted with an impulse to drop bricks on beetles and all other small crawly things. They may eventually wind up working for chemical companies, devising more sophisticated techniques of annihilation.
Roger Tory Peterson in *A Field Guide to Insects: America North of Mexico*, by Donald J. Borror and Richard E. White

Whirligigs (*Gyrinus*) float quietly on ponds and lakes—until disturbed—and then they whirl around erratically with the wild and crazy chaos of hundreds of bumper cars out of control. The group frenzy startles predators—or at least confuses them enough to buy the whirligigs some time.

How do these tiny whirling maniacs avoid colliding with each other? Special antennae, divided so that one part rests on the water, distinguishes its own ripples from its neighbors, enabling them to dodge the reflected ripples. They also have two sets of eyes, allowing them to see under- and out of water.

Not much bigger than a lady beetle, each tiny whirligig would be an easy meal for larger animals, but as a colony, the whirligigs together become a formidable defense system.

You started with a chaotic, irregular cloud of gas and dust, tumbling and contracting in the interstellar night. You ended with an elegant, jewel-like solar system, brightly illuminated, the individual planets neatly spaced out one from another, everything running like clockwork. The planets are nicely separated, you realize, because those that aren't are gone.

Carl Sagan and Ann Druyan in *Shadows of Forgotten Ancestors*

Giant water bugs (Belostomatidae) are the largest of the bugs living in ponds and streams. Their hind legs are used like paddles to swim. For air, they breathe through gills, which are two tubes at the tip of the abdomen.

In some species, females lay their eggs on the backs of the males, even though the eggs may be carrying the genetic traits of another male. A female can retain sperm from males with whom she mated prior to her current mate. Does the egg-carrying male "know" about her infidelities? To ensure that it is *his* sperm fertilizing his backpack of eggs, he mates with her just before she begins to lay eggs and continues to mate with her until she has laid her clutch. However, this is not always enough to stop stored sperm from another male from fertilizing her.

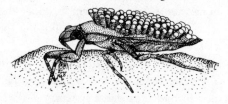

Giant water bugs eat by grasping prey such as fish and tadpoles with their strong front legs and inject a paralyzing venom into their bodies.

Through the puncture shoots the poisons that dissolve the victim's muscles and bones and organs—all but the victim's skin—and through it the giant water bug sucks out the victim's body. . . . The frog I saw was being sucked by a giant water bug . . . he slowly crumpled and began to sag. The spirit vanished from his eyes as if snuffed. His skin emptied and drooped . . . he was shrinking before my eyes like a deflated football.
Annie Dillard in *Pilgrim at Tinker Creek*

What's the difference between a **bug** and an **insect**? All bugs and insects have six legs and three body parts. A bug, however, also has a *rostrum*, a tubelike mouth used to suck up liquids either from a plant or an insect. An insect lacks this mouthpart and can consume solid as well as liquid food.

Those who study insects, entomologists, don't always agree on which is an insect or a bug, but all agree that the word *bug* in a name doesn't necessarily give it bug status.

The lightning bug, doodlebug, ladybug, pillbug and sowbug shown here (left) are *not* bugs (sowbugs and pillbugs aren't even insects, but rather crustaceans, related to crabs) but the insects to the right—water strider, green soldier, and aphids—*are* bugs.

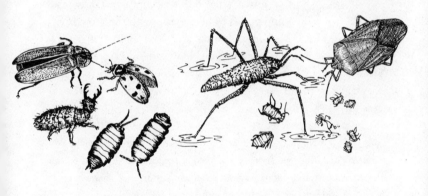

People who aren't entomologists sometimes think that the word "bug" is a little slangy, not latinate enough to be a scientific term, but it is.
Sue Hubbell in *Broadsides from the Other Orders*

The smallest of all plants are **algae**. Thousands of types of algae range in texture from the thick kelp mats in the ocean to the thin green paper used to wrap sushi.

In the summer, the surface film on ponds (*Spirogyra*) is one of the most familiar forms of algae. These algae are seen on quiet waters, often with tiny bubbles surrounding them, and an entourage of microscopic animals sucking up the oxygen from the bubbles.

Spirogyra spreads rapidly— its reproductive abilities are asexual and sexual. The asexual mode occurs constantly, causing ponds to be overrun with the growth. Sexual mating occurs when cells that are close enough fuse. Two filaments of this alga need to lie side by side to reproduce sexually, of course, but this is not always enough to lead to sex, for they must be of different mating types for reproduction to be successful.

Until about 600 million years ago, life on earth consisted of algae, bacteria and plankton. Then . . . in a burst of creativity lasting no more than 10 million years, nature produced an astonishing array of multicellular animals—the ancestors of virtually all creatures that now swim, fly, or crawl through the world.

J. Madeleine Nash in "When Life Exploded,"

Time, December 4, 1995

The flowers open as the sun rises and gradually close after a few hours, being
tightly closed at midday and at night. This pattern was interpreted as
the flower's ability to keep hidden and intact her innermost
secrets, invulnerable to hopeful invaders.

Anne McIntyre in *Flower Power*

$\mathcal{T}$he graceful floating flowers and pads of the **water lily**
(*Nymphaea*) commonly grow in ponds throughout North America.

Although most water lily flowers bloom during the day,
night-blooming species are encouraged to grow in backyard ponds
for their subtle sweet aroma. On summer nights the fragrance provides a relaxed atmosphere, giving many humans a feeling of well-
being. Night-pollinating insects are also attracted to the beautiful
flowers.

Our sense of smell is our primordial link to our brains. When we inhale a
scent, neurotransmitters in our brains trigger the production of biochemical
secretions that affect our moods, feelings, and emotions.

Sarah Ban Breathnach in *Simple Abundance*

Throughout the summer, beautiful yellow flowers of the **bladderwort** (*Utricularia cornuta*) bloom on the surface of ponds, bogs, marshes, and swamps. Below this quiet surface scene, a drama takes place in the thick tangle of the root system—no less intense than alligators stalking unsuspecting ducks: the air bladders on the roots devour passing animals by sucking them in with a powerful vacuumlike action.

Bladderworts get their nourishment by "eating" relatively huge creatures: insect larvae, drifting marine animals, and small fish. Little bladders attached to the roots have trapdoors that open automatically when food swims past. When larvae or fish approach, a vacuum sucks the animal into the bladder. The trapdoors are activated by sensitive trigger hairs that are activated, even by something as small as a mosquito larva. Once sucked in, the captured animal is dissolved by digestive enzymes. The bladder then closes up and resets itself for the next passerby.

Chance is always powerful. Let your hook be always cast;
in the pool where you least expect it, there will be a fish.
Ovid

Because **water hyacinths** (*Eichhornia*) grow quickly and abundantly, reproducing by the thousands each month, and because few animals are interested in eating them, they tend to choke our waterways. Their spectacular beauty doesn't override the damage caused to fish and other water creatures, so the battle between hyacinths and humans continues.

However, they may be used for positive results—they absorb nitrates and phosphates that cause algae bloom when water is deprived of oxygen. Also, the leaves and flower clusters of water hyacinths can be eaten—is this enough to suggest a kinder attitude toward them?

There are unknown forces within nature; when we give ourselves wholly to her, without reserve, she leads them to us; she shows us those forms which our watching eyes do not see, which our intelligence does not understand or suspect.
Auguste Rodin

*L*arge pale yellow flowers of the **lotus** (*Nelumbo lutea*) bloom on ponds and other quiet waters in the summer.

Hard seeds in segmented pods fall into the water, sometimes traveling to other parts of the waterway to take root. Once in a while the seeds lie dormant in mud or protected spots for centuries.

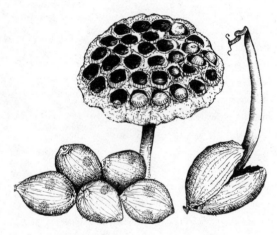

In 1995 scientists at UCLA sprouted a lotus seed almost 1,300 years old. Enzymes within the seed allowed it to survive thirteen centuries.

In a handful of wild seeds taken from any one natural community,
there is hidden the distillation of millions of years of coevolution of plants
and animals. . . . Is it not fitting that the lotus has become
associated with immortality?
Gary Nabhan in *Enduring Seeds*

Alderflies (*Sialis*) are not true flies, but related to a group of insects that includes antlions and lacewings. Alderflies spend their short lives of only two or three days without eating, simply crawling around leaves until they find a suitable spot near water to lay their eggs.

After locating a protected area, they lay several thousand cigar-shaped brown eggs. When all the eggs are laid, their mission is complete—and they die.

The larvae, however, despite the short life of adults, spend two to three years maturing. As newborns, they crawl to water, breathing through seven pairs of gills—those that aren't fast enough become fish food. After a few years, they change from monster-looking creatures with spikes into graceful winged adults. The mature alderfly shows no resemblance, either in looks or behavior, to the underwater creature it has been for the previous three years.

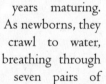

Just when we think we are clear about the direction of our lives, and we settle into that security (stagnation), something shakes our complacency. How much easier it is to recognize in the first place that life is a process and to open ourselves to the cycles of growth in ourselves.
Anne Wilson Schaef in *Meditations for Women Who Do Too Much*

When I was thirteen . . . I made a conscious effort to drop out of the race against night, knowing that for me there could be no such thing, in the conventional sense, as retirement, knowing that whether night arrived soon or late it would find me still flirting with words and with trouble.
E. B. White in *Race Against Night*

Raccoons (*Procyon lotor*) are the most urbanized wild creatures in our neighborhoods. They come out of their hidden homes at night to look for food in garbage cans, Dumpsters, streams, fields, farms, vacant lots, and riverbanks.

Raccoons grope in murky water for snails, clams, crabs, and fish, rolling their catch in their paws, appearing to wash their hands. They are, in fact, feeling their meal to "see" what it is. The water increases the sensitivity of their paws.

Living naturally as the animals do (not as city folk would call it) keeps me alert. No matter what the surprises or interferences, I can take them in stride. Because I am introverted and accustomed to isolated country, I take life the way a wild thing would: tired, I sleep; playful, I play; hungry, I eat. Like the animal, I am always up to date on my needs and keep close to myself. I can never get too much of this.
Jane Hollister Wheelwright in *The Long Shore*

Raccoons, although related to bears, don't hibernate. Rather, they go into a heavy sleep for long periods during the winter, living off their body fat.

Agile and deceptive, raccoons have adapted to living in cities and towns as easily as in the wild, using the darkness of night to sneak into garbage cans and pet food bowls. Unlike any other animal, they can get into closed containers by lifting lids, unscrewing hinges, and removing container seals. Their stealthy, secretive nature keeps them alive, allowing them to survive in areas where other animals would die.

But we're not satisfied with what we ourselves have learned about the world and ourselves. We're always waiting for a stranger to come and tell us something more. And "something more" means the rest of it.
Elio Vittorini

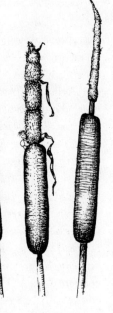

Common cattails (*Typha*) provide food all year round, not only for wildlife but also for humans. In winter, the roots can be eaten like potatoes, peeled and cooked, or made into a flour for baking. The sprouts can be steamed and the flower stalks eaten like mini ears of corn. Native Americans make a poultice from the roots to relieve pain and inflammation from wounds and burns.

Blackbirds peck at the cattails—not to eat, but to loosen the tightly packed seeds. Once free from their stalk, the seeds are light enough to travel through the air, gliding until they land in a good moist spot in a ditch, pond, or river.

I have come to understand that sacred plant medicine comes out of an
even deeper reality. That reality is encoded in the Native American concept
of Mother Earth and conveys in words the sense that the Earth is
a single living being and the life upon it her children.
Stephen Harrod Buhner in *Sacred Plant Medicine*

The distinctive calls of the male **red-winged blackbird** (*Agelaius phoeniceus*) are particularly loud and clear during mating season—as an indication of his territory's worth. Territory is an important clue for the female of his good genes.

During courtship, males expose the red patches that give them their name. The patches are hidden for most of the year under black feathers, and they generally have a yellow fringe, but in some western populations, the yellow is absent or inconspicuous.

Their red epaulet is also used to defend territory. Territory defense and courting are necessarily interwoven, not only with patch flashing, but also with song. One male can have as many as twelve females nesting simultaneously in his territory. As a rule, each male helps his first nesting female of the season feed her young, but not later ones. Females, too, will mate with other males when the opportunity for better genes presents itself.

Perhaps one in five of the matings that male Red-winged Blackbirds get on their territories may not be with their mates, and most Red-winged Blackbird nests contain young whose real fathers are the males in the territories next door. . . . Even among monogamous birds, though, a good deal of what ornithologists delicately call extra-pair copulation goes on. To put it bluntly, birds cheat and, we are now discovering, they cheat a lot.
Ronald Orenstein in *Songbirds*

Mating between **katydids** (*Microcentrum*) begins with the males sending out those familiar high-pitched summer noises—calls to females, asking, "Are you interested? Are you available? Where can I find you?" Some katydid females answer back with clicks of their own, an unusual occurrence in the animal world, since females usually don't participate in love songs.

The sounds guide them to each other. If the female is receptive, foreplay begins with antennae stroking and maneuvering around each other. If she remains interested, the female accepts a gift of a protein snack presented by the male along with his package of sperm. His fitness as a sperm donor is reflected in the gift, so if he's strong and fit, he'll be a good investment for her. He gives her the best he can to ensure his genes will be passed on.

Although their song certainly draws us, conveying as it does warmth, summer, and the friendliness of nighttime, I suspect part of their appeal is aesthetic. Katydids are beautiful. . . . They are big, plump, jolly-looking bugs in nursery-bright green, a couple of inches long.
Sue Hubbell in *Broadsides from the Other Orders*

Nighthawks (*Chordeiles minor*) are neither hawks as their common name implies, nor are they "minor," as their scientific name suggests; the only other nighthawk in their genus is actually smaller.

However, they *are* night birds. They begin feeding after sunset by swooping after insects. Known as "flying insect traps," they buzz through the night skies hunting for swarms of insects, catching them in their huge, gaping mouths. Bristles around the nighthawk's beak protect its eyes as it flies into the thick clouds of insects.

Nighthawks, of course, sleep all day, camouflaged by their mottled "dead leaf" plumage, inconspicuous on the sun-flecked branches where they roost.

If this night bird were captured and forced to sleep during the night, would we call it an insomniac bird because it wouldn't sleep according to our schedule? A biological clock isn't a specific organ that can be reset like a watch. Rather, the timing mechanism is dispersed through every cell of a body.

We have no data on the exact number of delayed sleep phase
syndrome sufferers, but the lack of public awareness of the syndrome
dooms them all to a frustrating conflict with society.
Peretz Lavie in *The Enchanted World of Sleep*

*I*n the fifth century, Hippocrates noted that malaria, a scourge for thousands of years, inflicted people mostly around marshy areas, and not the inland residents. He concluded the problem was the "bad air"—*mal aria* of the marsh.

Female **mosquitoes** (Culicidae) are attracted to the warm moist areas of marshes, ponds, lakes—anywhere warm water is available for them to lay eggs.

The whining from mosquitoes is made by the female's wings and picked up by the male's sensitive antennae with thousands of fine tiny hairs that receive the vibrations. He uses these signals to find her to mate.

After mating, he takes off, probably to die, and she settles down to lay her eggs in the still, quiet water they need to survive.

> *In these formal ways, men and women domesticate their emotional*
> *lives. But their strategies are different, their biological itineraries are different.*
> *His sperm needs to travel, her egg needs to settle down. It's*
> *astonishing that they survive happily at all.*
> Diane Ackerman in *A Natural History of Love*

*B*oth male and female **mosquitoes** feed on nectar for nourishment, but only females need the protein in blood to manufacture eggs.

A female mosquito chisels her way through animal flesh until blood vessel walls are broken. Normally coagulation would begin, but, because she also injects a blood-thinning liquid, the blood flows easily—into her and into the eggs in her abdomen. The blood-thinning substance also contains single-celled fungi that irritate the surrounding tissue of our skin; hence, the itch. It is this irritation that draws blood to the area.

The familiar itchy swelling is our body's reaction to the chemical, but it takes almost a minute to occur, so by the time we slap at the irritating bump, the mosquito is usually off on another errand of blood-sucking.

We swat ploddingly—and are likely to kill only the slowest feeders.
Thus we do our bit for natural selection, helping ensure that future generations
come only from mosquitoes that are quick enough to get away
with our blood in a minute or less.

Richard Conniff in "Body Beasts," *National*
Geographic, December 1998

*F*emale **mosquitoes** lay eggs on quiet water; newly hatched larvae need to breathe in undisturbed water. They hang, head down, and breathe through tubes at the tail end of their bodies, which stick out from the water's surface.

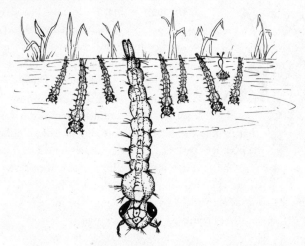

At this stage, millions of larvae are eaten by small fish, bladderworts, birds, crustaceans—they are the Pablum of the water world, and the substance that will become food for the larger animals: trout, bass, raccoons, herons, eagles, and humans.

It was given to us by the creator to take care of the Earth. Every time we speak, we speak for tree, water, fish. . . . We put ourselves in a humble position, no greater than bird or duck or plant. We're as humble as they are. I look at the mountain as if my life depends on it—for food, medicine—not just to see how beautiful it is. The animals can't speak for themselves, so we speak for them.

Sarah James in "First People," by Linda Hogan from *Intimate Nature*

With their long pointy wings, swifts are some of the fastest fliers of all birds, covering thousands of miles between their summer and winter homes. They fly at speeds clocked at over one hundred miles per hour. The **chimney swift** (*Chaetura pelagica*) flies most of the day eating insects on the fly without stopping to rest. To drink, they dip into ponds or streams as they fly over them.

At night, swifts stop flying and roost on vertical surfaces of buildings and, of course, chimneys. Why do they use chimneys? Before humans were around, the swifts built their homes in large hollow trees in forests. When the forest trees were cut to build houses, the swifts adapted by using the human architecture, which served as well; the chimneys were the highest vertical surface—an adequate substitute for tree trunks.

Chimney swifts use their small feet and the sharp tips of their tail feathers to cling when roosting or building nests. Nests are made from small twigs glued together with their saliva. Both male and female have large salivary glands, which enlarge during nesting. They cover each twig with the gluelike saliva so each one sticks easily in the nest. Birds' nest soup in Asia is made from swifts' nests built entirely from the protein-rich saliva.

Original details are very ordinary, except to the mind that sees their extraordinariness. It's not that we need to go to the Hopi mesas to see greatness; we need to view what we already have in a different way.
Natalie Goldberg in *Writing Down the Bones*

*. . . It has no special value to humans. It is neither despised as a weed
nor exploited for its usefulness . . . we should take its name to heart and treat
it—and all its wildflower companions—as sacred, respecting their
existence and protecting them from harm for their own sake.*
Barbara Burn in *North American Wildflowers*

*T*all spikes of **vervain** (*Verbena hastata*) are covered
with beautiful violet-blue flowers that bloom
through the summer in fields, roadsides, and
stream banks.

Nowadays, vervain is considered a
weed by most, but the ancient Greeks
revered it as a sacred plant with healing
powers to relieve stomach disorders and tension headaches. Native Americans still revere it
for its healing abilities.

*Vervain helps these people to use their huge resources of
energy in a more natural way. Dr. Bach said, "vervain
teaches us that it is by being rather than by doing that great
things are accomplished." It engenders a calm and open
attitude to the ideas of others, and allows their
exuberance to be an inspiration to others. It helps
towards a more balanced and harmonious
life, treading the Middle Path.*
Anne McIntyre in *Flower Power*

What's going on in the head of a sparrow while chirping and trilling? In many songbirds, like this **chipping sparrow** (*Spizella passerina*), the corpus callosum, the link between the sides of the brain, is thicker in females than in males, even as embryos. With this thicker bridge, images can process faster and easier between lobes. Robert Bly in *Men* 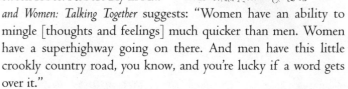 *and Women: Talking Together* suggests: "Women have an ability to mingle [thoughts and feelings] much quicker than men. Women have a superhighway going on there. And men have this little crookly country road, you know, and you're lucky if a word gets over it."

A female sparrow learns to recognize the songs of her neighbors while still in the nest. Although not singers themselves, females must "learn" the songs so they can avoid mating with males who sound too much like their own fathers, while ignoring songsters whose repertoires are too unfamiliar from the dialect of the local population.

The problem may be that each partner is operating within a different system, speaking a different genderlect. . . . Understanding genderlects makes it possible to change—to try speaking differently—when you want to.
Deborah Tannen in *You Just Don't Understand*

Appetite and sex are the great motivators of history.
Isabel Allende in *Aphrodite*

Generally, **spiders** eat anything smaller than themselves, which creates a problem for males, who are almost always smaller than females.

How then does a male approach a female? In some species, males present a gift of a silk-wrapped insect. He carries the gift, holding it in front of his body as he tentatively moves closer until she takes it from him with her fangs. This way, her defense system is occupied long enough for him to climb on her to mate. This doesn't always work, as is nature's way, and a male with an empty package or too small of a gift will be eaten on the spot with no chance to escape.

Animals have much to teach us about our own romantic habits. There are many parallels. Male animals often give the equivalent of engagement rings, females often check a male's bank balance, and "modesty" or "playing coy" is as much a trump card for female birds or insects or reptiles as for humans.
Diane Ackerman in *A Natural History of Love*

$\mathcal{B}$ig and beautiful with clear wings and red eyes, **cicadas** (Magicicada) are sometimes confused with locusts. But cicadas are non-jumping insects, and make a loud whining noise unlike any other wildlife.

Their high-pitched sounds come only from the males and only during their summer courtship. Vibrations, created from an elaborate and powerful muscle on the male's abdomen, are carried over long distances through the summer air to females, who receive the signals with sensitive ears on their bellies. The females can identify the species by the frequency of the signals.

When males and females congregate for mating, it's usually by the thousands, simultaneously. Their numbers alone ward off predators and they reproduce abundantly for several weeks during late summer.

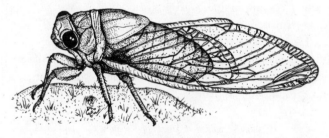

Its noise is hard to describe; there is nothing like it in nature that I have heard. Imagine a whine, the sound of a power saw going on at high speed into a cracked board. You can't tell, when you hear the cicada, just where its whine comes from, for it seems to be everywhere, like air turned to sound.

Castle Freeman, Jr., in *Spring Snow*

---

*F*emale **cicadas** die after laying hundreds of eggs in trees and shrubs. A few weeks later, nymphs from the eggs drop to the ground, enter the soil, and live in chambers near the trees' roots.

Depending on the species, these nymphs live underground for up to seventeen years, until, as if prompted by an internal guidance, they start climbing their way up through the soil. When they are close to the surface, they wait until evening, when it's cooler and safer, to emerge.

The new cicadas then climb onto nearby trees and buildings to perform an act so remarkable it can't be even closely duplicated in the most technologically advanced laboratories—a perfectly formed mature animal casually walks out of itself, leaving behind the skin of its former being, the only evidence of its long underground development.

> *We must be willing to get rid of the life we've planned,*
> *so as to have the life that is waiting for us.*
> Joseph Campbell

Pansies (*Viola*) are related to violets, the result of crossbreeding four different *viola* species in the early 1800s. An English gardener experimented for thirty years before developing the colorful velvety pansy.

They bloom in the spring and last for months, providing edible leaves to eat through the summer. Seeds develop inside protective pods as shown here.

The name pansy comes from the French *pensée*, meaning "thought." The French gave pansies to their lovers to remind them to think of the giver.

So many people walk around with a meaningless life. They seem half-asleep, even when they're busy doing things they think are important. This is because they're chasing the wrong things. The way you get meaning in your life is to devote yourself to loving others, devote yourself to your community around you, and devote yourself to creating something that gives you purpose and meaning.

Morrie Schwartz, in *Tuesdays with Morrie*, by Mitch Albom

The large webbed feet of **ducks** paddle alternately—like canoers rather than rowers. Their feet spread out for the power stroke, then fold up for the recovery stroke—a lot of motion underwater without showing any exertion from above. Ducks floating calmly on a pond are the epitome of serenity, but their continuous efforts, unseen above the surface, are constant and powerful—even when they simply stay in place.

When you are in doubt, be still, and wait. When doubt no longer exists for you, then go forward with courage. So long as mists envelop you, be still; be still until the sunlight pours through and dispels the mists—as it surely will. Then act with courage.
White Eagle

August 8

Remember that searching out the significance of Nature's expression to you is a way of honoring it.
Ted Andrews in *Animal-Speak*

*I*n the summer, the flowers of **blazing stars** (*Liatris*) begin to open from the top of the stem down—rather than from the bottom up as is the way with most other stalked plants. Because of this and their big purple flower heads, they stand out among the other roadside and field wildflowers.

There is a strong and powerful life force that moves within the bodies of the wild plants. But I saw that—in spite of the work human beings had done in the genetic development of plants species—what they have created does not carry that life force as strongly. I wonder now, as I did then, how is it that we have come to accept this dilution of life force in what we create as a normal thing?
Stephen Harrod Buhner in *Sacred Plant Medicine*

Moonflowers (*Ipomoea alba*) open only at night—each flower just for one night—to reveal their fragrance as it unfurls its petals in the dark. Night-blooming flowers are typically bright white to catch the attention of their pollinators, night-flying moths.

After sunrise, when light starts to shine on them, they close—about the same time the similar-looking morning glories begin to open.

The extreme variations of biological clocks among humans shouldn't be surprising when we see it throughout nature, in all species, including flowers.

Remember Mother Nature's role in the scheme of things. The perfume that fills the night air was not intended for human enjoyment, but rather to attract nocturnal pollinators, such as moths and bats, to the plants.
Cathy Wilkinson Barash in *Evening Gardens*

Slugs, with no shell to cover their sensitive bodies, are vulnerable to the sun's drying rays. To avoid daylight they emerge and forage for food only in the safety of night. Hormonal levels change during their twenty-four-hour cycle, just as humans' hormone and temperature levels rise and fall according to their biological schedules.

For some humans with biological clocks out of sync with a day schedule, wake-up calls are obviously difficult. Complaints from night people, insomniacs, new parents, light sleepers, and nappers illustrate the lifelong struggle to adjust to an unnatural cycle.

Alarm clock awakenings for night people, when our hormone levels are peaking for deepest sleep, are no less difficult than requiring us to stop a speeding train by standing in front of it. Sometimes even the anticipation of oncoming pain clouds the pleasure of sleep.

Three forms of adjustment to earth's rotation developed during the evolutionary process: that of nocturnal animals whose activity begins with the setting of the sun; that of daylight animals who come to life at sunrise; and that of animals who are active twice a day. . . . It is quite amazing that recognition of the importance of biological clocks took such a long time.
Peretz Lavie in *The Enchanted World of Sleep*

*S*lugs are mollusks, one of the first forms of animal life to live on land. In Spanish, slugs are called *babosas,* from the verb meaning "to drool." Slime, secreted from a gland under the slug's head, flows down to a muscular "foot" and allows them to glide over surfaces as they travel.

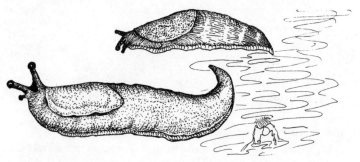

A shiny trail of mucus on sidewalks and roads is a good indication that a slug has traveled down that path. Their slime not only protects the slugs from cuts and wounds, it also gives them protection from diseases. Scientists have discovered medicinal benefits for humans from slug's slime for mucus-related diseases such as cystic fibrosis.

What we are now learning about animals returns us to a world so powerfully beyond our contemporary imaginations that we have almost missed it. . . .
Linda Hogan in "First People," from *Intimate Nature*

*F*inding a partner and mating in the dark is no problem for **slugs**. Their eyes are at the tops of their tentacles, and in some species the tentacles also function as infrared receptors, letting them "see" the heat of other creatures in the dark.

After finding a mate, *Limax*, a common slug, climbs a tree with its partner. Together they make a dramatic leap, intertwined and suspended by threads of mucus. These original bungee-jumpers mate with their bodies tightly connected, in midair, exchanging sperm. Sometimes they remain like this through the night, ensuring the sperm transfer and their genes passing to the next generation.

Slugs' biological clocks are scheduled to mate in the summer so when they produce eggs in August, the young will have an abundance of food.

When a man and a woman hungrily push their bodies together, they are not thinking about evolution, even if they're scientists. At the tremulous moment of orgasm, a man's thoughts usually are not about passing on his genes.
Dean Hamer in *Living with Our Genes*

Everything begins with a thought. . . . We become what we think about.
If we don't think at all, we don't become anything at all.
Earl Nightingale in *Earl Nightingale's Greatest Discovery*

Sandspurs (*Cenchrus*) grow profusely in sandy areas, while **cockle-burs** (*Xanthium*) need rich soil to thrive. But both have evolved a system to spread themselves by hitchhiking on the fur and skin of mammals.

Tiny hooks cover the seed pods; when a human or animal walks by, the seeds easily cling to fur, skin, or socks—ready to travel to new territory.

In the middle 1900s, George de Mestral, a Swiss scientist, be-came fascinated with the seeds sticking to his clothes whenever he re-turned from walks in nearby fields. Look-ing at the stickers under his microscope, he noticed the tiny hooks, and his mind started looking for ways to use nature's idea. Eight years later he applied the hitchhiker-hook technology to fasten-ers and came up with the idea for Velcro.

Seeds on the coyote's tail, seeds on the hunter's coat, thistledown mounting on the winds—all were somehow triumphing over life's limitations.
Loren Eiseley in *How Flowers Changed the World*

No-see-ums (*Culicoides*) (shown left) are the size of a point of a pin—almost microscopic, hence their name. They are small enough to fly through screen mesh and nets, but their bite, a hot painful slash, is far out of proportion to their size. No-see-ums swarm around human bodies and inject thousands of tiny burning pricks—evidence of their presence without being seen.

No-see-ums, or punkies, are just one of many species of **biting midges**. Like mosquitoes, they suck blood to nourish their eggs, but no-see-ums have mouths that *cut* into flesh, rather than the *piercing* mouths of mosquitoes.

Some other **midge** species (shown right), however, are incapable of biting. They are nectar and sap feeders and don't have the mouthparts needed to slash through flesh like the no-see-ums. Swarms of them, flying cloudlike around human heads, are mildly irritating, but never outrageously painful as are the biting midges.

Midges gather by "swarm markers," certain spots in the air that designate their territory. Midges are usually in the same area each day around the same time during the spring and summer. If a human walks into their territory, the midges are likely to adopt the large body as their swarm marker and follow for a distance. Swarms help males and females find each other.

The meeting of two personalities is like contact of two chemical substances:
if there is any reaction, both are transformed.
Carl Jung

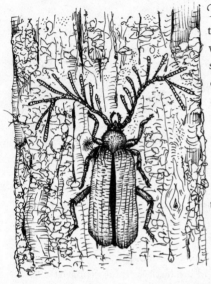

Fire beetles (*Pyrochroidae*) are active in June and July on tree bark, where the female lays eggs. Their scientific name means "fire-colored"—hot reds, yellows, and oranges contrast against the brown background of bark, soil, and leaves.

During courtship, a male fire beetle displays a cleft in his forehead to get a female's attention. If the cleft is suitable to the female, she grabs his head, licks the cleft, and then allows him to mate with her.

*In the courtship behavior of a beetle species called Pyrochroidae,
for example, the male beetle goes through a bizarre ritual of displaying to a
potential mate a deep cleft in his forehead. The meaning of that cleavage had long
been elusive, but scientists now know that it encloses a tempting sample,
a small dose of the chemical caxtharidin, familiarly known as
Spanish Fly. During courtship, she grabs his head and
immediately laps up the chemical offering with the cleft.
Apparently impressed with the hors d'oeuvre,
she allows the male to mate. . . .*

Natalie Angier in *The Beauty of the Beastly*

Sunflowers (*Helianthus*) are symbolic of happiness because their faces are always pointing up toward the sun. Paradoxically, sunlight inhibits stem growth, so the shaded side of the stem grows faster, tipping the flower's head toward the sun, giving the impression the flower heads are sunning themselves.

Sunflowers have an incredible ability to absorb water. Their long, persistent roots travel deep into sandy soil to find moisture. In Russia, Turkey, and Persia, sunflowers were planted to reduce malaria—the sunflowers eliminated wet areas where the malaria-causing mosquitoes thrived.

In addition to helping control insect populations, sunflowers are valued for food and are grown worldwide for their seeds. All our common plant food comes from plants that have flowers to attract pollinators.

It would have been a very different world if early flowering plants . . . had not been successful. There would have been no apples, no Wheaties in the morning, no corn on the cob, no potatoes, no rice or other grains.

David Dilcher, *Palm Beach Post*, November 27, 1998

*P*ulling out **dandelions** as weeds and tossing them aside won't stop their life cycle. The seeds are so light they can be carried through the air with the smallest puff of wind. They stay in the air as long as the humidity is low—then, strategically, when humidity rises preceding a rain, they lose their height and fall to the ground.

Each seed has hooklike hairs at the end that help attach itself to a passing animal or to the soil once it lands.

The word *dandelion* comes from the French for "lion's tooth," *dent de lion*, referring to the shape of the leaves.

Almost all parts of a dandelion can be eaten—they have a high concentration of vitamins C and B_2. Tea is brewed from the leaves to relieve cold symptoms. The tea is also used as a diuretic to relieve fluid retention without depleting the body of potassium. Young leaves can be cooked and eaten like spinach or mixed raw with salads. Many Native and non-Native Americans eat the fleshy roots like potatoes, peeled, sliced, and boiled. The only part of a dandelion that shouldn't be eaten is the stem.

A weed is no more than a flower in disguise.
James Russell Lowell

I have learned that what I have not drawn I have never really seen, and that when I start drawing an ordinary thing I realize how extraordinary it is, sheer miracle: the branching of a tree, the structure of a dandelion's puff.

Frederick Franck in *The Zen of Seeing*

Dandelion pollen is light and tough, as are most pollens, and can last for years without losing its ability to pollinate. Everything about the dandelion is made for survival—no other weed is more successful.

A dandelion's life history strategy is to reproduce as rapidly as possible. These plants quickly fill an environment—a newly plowed field, for example—before the environment changes—that is, before winter comes, before the corn grows too large, or before the farmer plows again.

John Postlethwait and Janet Hopson
in *The Nature of Life*

$\mathcal{A}$ccording to studies by research biologist Bruce Bagemihl, homosexual behavior occurs in more than 450 different kinds of animals worldwide, and it is far more common than previously recognized or reported.

Among **Canada geese** (*Branta canadensis*) homosexual parents are generally as good at parenting as heterosexual ones. Examples of same-sex pairs successfully raising young have been documented in at least twenty species, and in a few cases, homosexual couples actually appear to have an advantage over heterosexual ones.

In most species the same courtship behaviors are used in both homosexual and heterosexual interactions. Sometimes, however, same-sex courtship involves only a subset of the movements and behaviors found in opposite-sex displays. For example, when Canada Geese court each other homosexually, they perform a neck-dipping ritual also found in heterosexual courtships, but do not adopt the special posture that males and females use after mating.

Bruce Bagemihl in *Biological Exuberance*

$\mathcal{A}$ female **trap-door spider** (*Bothriocyrtum californicum*) digs a burrow about six inches into soft ground, lining the walls with silk. A lid is built to fit neatly over the opening, made from nearby material and underlined with gravel so it falls shut under its own weight.

She stays hidden inside by day until dark, when she lifts the trapdoor slightly to peek out. To catch food, she simply reaches out her four front legs and waits for an insect to pass, which she pulls in, the trapdoor closing automatically behind her. She never needs to leave the safety of her underground home.

Males, who have their own burrows, only venture out to visit females. After mating, they return to their own burrows.

"Mating" means that the chromosomes of the two spiders "line up" and exchange a portion of their length. This sounds bizarre and contrived until you remember that it is exactly what real chromosomes, of ourselves as well as spiders, actually do in sexual reproduction.
Richard Dawkins in *Climbing Mount Improbable*

$\int$yrphid flies (*Metasyrphus*) look like bees, but hover like hummingbirds near flowers, which they pollinate—almost as reliably as bees. Bees have four wings, but syrphid flies have only two. Their wings and ability to hover give them their common name, hover fly.

Despite the bright yellow-and-black wasp-look of their abdomen, syrphid flies can't sting or bite. Their disguise allows them to fly freely from flower to flower without harm from predators such as birds.

The larvae, however, are nondescript grubs that aggressively attack aphids, hoisting them over their heads like tiny weight lifters, using their mouthparts to hold them in midair as they eat. Several weeks and hundreds of aphids later, each larva pupates, changing from a chubby grub to a convincingly beelike animal.

Some syrphid flies buzz rather like bees, and some of the species are patterned in
yellow and black and so resemble bees that people are afraid of them, but they
have no stingers and can do no harm . . . but bugs are good liars. In fact, lying
is one of the things they do best—it's a way they keep from being killed and
thus pass along their genes. Their exuberant, built-in biological lying earns the
admiration and respect of those of us who have to make up our paltry falsehoods
consciously and laboriously with whatever scraps we can gather.

Sue Hubbell in *Broadsides from the Other Orders*

The "autumn migration" of many birds actually starts well before autumn. In July and August several species begin their yearly journey south.

The **red-eyed vireo** (*Vireo olivaceus*) is one of the earliest of the long-distance migratory birds. Both eastern and western species of songbirds leave their homes long before food runs out or weather turns cold. Many species linger along the way taking longer than needed, perhaps as insurance just in case weather turns unexpectedly or perhaps to research new areas for the future since the trend of seasonal climates has been changing.

> *What is our commonest bird in America? Is it the robin? I doubt it.*
> *I would not be at all surprised to find that in the eastern states, at least, the*
> *red-eyed vireo is more numerous than the robin. Yet everyone knows the*
> *familiar robin and only those interested in birds know the vireo.*
> *The reason is that the robin, found around the doorstep, is seen by everyone.*
> *On the other hand, it is very thinly distributed in the more wooded*
> *sections. Just the opposite is true of the red-eye.*
> Roger Tory Peterson in *Birds Over America*

Spiders taste with organs in their feet. The end segment of a spider's leg, which has several holes containing taste and smell organs, is called a *tarsus.*

Spiders also use their feet and legs to communicate—the tug and pull on a female's web by a male says more than paragraphs do for some humans: a series of tugs says: "I'm a strong male with great genes coming to see if you're interested...." Whether she responds depends on his strength, or perhaps his persistence and quickness.

Among humans, when a boy tugs on a ponytail in the playground, the girl's response depends on the feel of the tug and who the tugger is.

> *The female's heart-strings are of taut, well-tempered silk. If a male wishes to woo her and avoid, or at least postpone, being eaten, he had best play upon those strings. Orpheus himself had not better cause. In some cases the male stations himself right at the edge of the female's web and plucks the web as one might pluck a harp.*
> Richard Dawkins in *Climbing Mount Improbable*

The **praying mantis** (*Mantis religiosa*) is a symbol of the power of stillness and patience. According to many Native Americans, whenever Mantis got himself into trouble, he would go off to be alone. He would then go to sleep and wait for the solution to his problem to come to him.

With remarkable stillness, instead of hunting, the praying mantis waits for food to come to him; at the exact right moment, after not moving for a long time, the mantis reaches out a long spiny foreleg to grasp an insect who walked or flew by just a little too close. Anyone who has swatted flies knows the speed needed to hit them, let alone clutch one sandwich-style the way the praying mantis can.

A female may eat the head of her sex partner, probably to increase her level of protein, calories, and nutrients so she'll produce healthy offspring.

Mantises have been around for millions of years and it may take us a few decades more before we can fully resolve the challenge posed by the occasional occurrence of cannibalism by mating females. While we work on this mystery, may the survivors sow what they can on our behalf in the garden, waiting patiently in a prayerful mode for a pest to come their way.

John Alcock in *In a Desert Garden*

---

*F*lies react to rapid motion but can't detect slow-moving objects. When a praying mantis or lizard catches a fly, it's usually after a long and extremely slow approach. The brains of flies, although sophisticated in other behaviors, simply don't process slow movements.

Their own approach to food is an automatic response to a depleted sugar level, which triggers a solution: fly around until food is detected. Their familiar zigzag flight is their way of hunting, and when food is sensed, the fly lands near it. The fly then walks until it locates a meal, usually carbohydrates. It sucks the food with its proboscis—if it isn't sweet enough, oral receptors shut down, and the fly receives a signal to look elsewhere for a better solution.

When the fly finds a good meal, it continues to feed until nerve fibers send a signal to stop. In laboratory experiments, when those nerve fibers were cut, the fly would eat nonstop, and literally blow itself up from eating more food than would fit in its body.

If it's not delicious, don't eat it.
Sarah Ban Breathnach in *Simple Abundance*

Kingfishers (*Megaceryle alcyon*) beat their wings like hummingbirds, use their bills like woodpeckers, cast pellets like owls, and build their nests in tunnels in riverbanks—like no other bird. In keeping with their nonconformist behavior, female kingfishers are more colorful than the males, and they forage for food for the young—typically a male bird's job.

To catch fish, kingfishers dive from perches or hover twenty or so feet above water before grabbing small fish with their powerful bills. They return to their perches to beat the fish against a tree, then flip it in the air and swallow it headfirst as it comes back down.

They live alone except during breeding when pairs stay together, living in long, horizontal tunnels cut into the banks of streams and rivers. After breeding, pairs separate, leaving the chicks—and resume their solitary life.

> *Individuals with kingfishers as a totem need to be close to the water, preferably as far north as possible. . . . The kingfisher is a bold bird that fishes for its living. . . . Its ability to draw life out of the waters to feed itself reflects the kingfisher's ability to stimulate new opportunities for prosperity. Often it requires that you dive headlong into some activity, but it usually proves to be very beneficial.*
> Ted Andrews in *Animal-Speak*

*I*nstead of nests, **kingfishers** build horizontal tunnels in the banks of rivers and streams. Similar to woodpeckers, they use their bills like jackhammers, pounding to break into a surface. They attack the bank until a hole is formed. Then, unlike any other bird, they dig out dirt with their feet, shoveling away until a deep tunnel is made, just wide enough for them to crawl into. At the end of the tunnel, a "turnaround" chamber is excavated, where the eggs will be laid.

Both parents provide food for the chicks, who eat their parents' partially digested fish. But often, the male contributes much more time and energy than the female in raising the young. The female, on the other hand, spends more time than the male on territorial defense.

Courtship feeding is part of the courting ritual of a male kingfisher when he carries food to the female before she lays her eggs. The amount of courtship feeding may be a way for the female to determine if the male will be a good provider for their chicks. Courtship feeding continues even after they have bonded, to improve the healthy production of eggs.

True intuition is subtle and graceful and will leave you secure if you listen.
Sonia Choquette in *The Psychic Pathway*

Some flowers are pollinated by insects, some by wind, and some by both. **Dog fennel** (*Eupatorium capillifolium*) evolved to use both methods. They bloom in the late summer, when swarms of insects are available to carry pollen; and the oncoming change in season provides breezes to carry the pollen by air. Nature uses whatever works.

The pollen is almost indistinguishable from ragweed pollen, which is responsible for most allergy problems in the summer.

We do not know what we are and cannot agree on what we want to be. The primary cause of this intellectual failure is ignorance of our origins. We did not arrive on this planet as aliens. Humanity is part of nature, a species that evolved among other species. The more closely we identify ourselves with the rest of life, the more quickly we will be able to discover sources of human sensibility....

Edward O. Wilson in *The Diversity of Life*

Normally **songbirds** are active by day and rest at night, but just before migrating their regular sleep pattern is disrupted by *Zugunruhe*. This German term describes a twice-yearly cycle of nocturnal restlessness that occurs when songbirds are stimulated and conditioned to migrate. The length of the restlessness varies in proportion to the length of the migration. Even when caged, migrating songbirds become fitful—hopping and jumping from perch to perch at the onset of the migratory season.

Genetically programmed to follow a particular direction and to start the migration at a particular time, songbirds face the direction of their impending journey even without any clues such as stars to orient themselves.

Many humans not only deal with periods of restless leg syndrome, they also experience disrupted sleep patterns in sporadic bouts during the fall and spring.

Another unpredictable group are the late migrants, or lingerers, as they are sometimes called. Many birds seem to wait too long and lose the urge to migrate. Others are trapped by early snowstorms and are obliged to stay behind. It is not that they are incapacitated. Low fat reserves and lowered vitality may simply mean that they are poorly fitted to undertake the long flight southward.

John V. Dennis in *A Complete Guide to Bird Feeding*

When a bird grows fidgety prior to a storm, it may be responding to the increased positive ions in the air—which modify the brain's serotonin levels. Humans may feel depressed or anxious just before a storm without understanding the cause. Are humans influenced by the same bioelectric stimulation as birds? Determining environmental influences on moods is as difficult as measuring the gravitational pull on a feather—too small to easily calculate, but too relevant to ignore.

Birds respond to the weather, light, and air changes between seasons. Eating, mating, plumage, and migration are affected. **Summer tanagers** (*Piranga rubra*) arrive in the United States in the summer (hence, their name) to begin breeding. Their colors change as a result of molting—old feathers are replaced by new ones. Males complete their molt with a bright-red plumage in time for courting. Typical of all songbirds, tanagers begin singing at the onset of the breeding season, fully dressed for the occasion.

However reassuring it may be to think of birds as greeting card caricatures— plump, rosy, and smiling—it is doubtful that entertaining humans or expressing its feelings of happiness is the motivation behind a bird's song. In a sense, a singing bird is communicating that it is healthy, strong, and in possession of a territory.
Lester L. Short in *The Lives of Birds*

Wild parrots in urban areas are usually "escapes" (*not* "escapees") from houses and apartments. The **blue-crowned conure** (*Aratinga acuticaudata*) shown here is a common escape in the south. Flocks containing dozens of the colorful conures swoop into backyards, cavorting like wild mariachi bands. They land together in tall trees, and as if on cue, fall silent and disappear in the leaves. This time is often spent grooming their feathers.

Preening is an important part of all birds' routine. Feathers need to be cleaned, oiled, and straightened out, most of which is done by running their beaks through the feathers. Not only dirt, but fungi, lice, bacteria, and feather mites can be irritating if not fatal to the bird. Some of the parasites have parasites of their own, and at times, one single bird can be a huge community of miniature populations.

A single parrot species, the green conure of Mexico, is host to as many as thirty species, each with four life stages, making a total of over a hundred life forms. Each of these forms in turn has its own preferred site and pattern of behavior. A single conure harbors fifteen or more species of feather mites, with seven occupying different sites on the individual feather.
Edward O. Wilson in *The Diversity of Life*

The **barn spider** (*Araneus cavaticus*) is the main character in E. B. White's *Charlotte's Web*. Charlotte spins at night like other orb weavers. She stays in the middle of the web until daylight, when she moves to a retreat out of sight.

The Dakotas believe that a perfect orb web symbolizes the beauty of the heavens.

> *Spider is the guardian of the ancient languages and alphabets. . . . To many there was an alphabet even more primordial. It was formed by the geometric patterns and angles found within spider's web. To many this was the first true alphabet. This is why spider is considered the teacher of language and the magic of writing.*
> Ted Andrews in *Animal-Speak*

Several species of evening primrose bloom on summer evenings, but their name is misleading, as they aren't actually primroses, nor do all evening primroses open in the evening. Many open in the day or late at night, and some, known as sun-drops, bloom in the morning.

The **common evening primrose** (*Oenothera biennis*), shown here, opens after sunset from June through September in fields, gardens, lawns, and roadsides.

Native Americans use the roots to make a tea that soothes stomachaches. The seed oil helps skin problems like eczema and redness. The oil is a source for omega fatty acids, which are vital for healthy functioning of the immune, nervous, and hor-monal systems. Another fatty acid in evening primroses is impor-tant in balancing PMS, hyperactivity, migraines, arthritis, and high blood pressure.

Mind energy which vibrates so fast that it appears invisible is therefore not so different from a flower, or a tree, or even a rock that vibrates so slowly we may not recognize its essential dynamism. This may go a long way to explaining the deep connection we feel to the plant world.
Anne McIntyre in *Flower Power*

*We are at our human finest, dancing with our minds, when there are
more choices than two. Sometimes there are ten, even twenty different ways
to go, all but one bound to be wrong, and the richness of selection
in such situations can lift us onto totally new ground.*
Lewis Thomas in *The Medusa and the Snail*

Skippers are named for their energetic darting flight, skipping
from flower to flower. Each has a dance of its own, and colors that
range from iridescent aqua to dull yellows and browns.

Are skippers moths or butterflies? Skippers
have both moth and butterfly characteristics—
stocky, hairy bodies with short wings like
moths; but they are active during
the day like butterflies.
As is nature's way of
keeping us guessing and
open-minded, not all skippers are hairy and some don't
even skip during the day. Some
professionals classify them with
moths, but not all agree. They
have been granted their own
superfamily name, Hesperioidea.

*Everyone has a talent. What is rare is the courage to follow the
talent to the dark place where it leads.*
Erica Jong

September 4

$Pillbugs$ (*Armadillium*) are nocturnal little crustaceans, related to lobsters and crabs, but able to live on land. Commonly called rolypolies, pillbugs can roll themselves into tight little balls, not only for defense, but also to hold moisture needed for survival; 400 million years ago, they left the sea and their crustacean relatives to become land dwellers. They still depend on gills to breathe, and get their oxygen from the water retained in their armorlike covering.

Sowbugs are similar to pillbugs, but can't roll into balls. Both stay hidden during the day and both will eat almost anything available, including roots, fungi, plants, seedlings, and droppings from insects, spiders, and birds.

Survivors in their changing environment, pillbugs can even transform their gender. French researchers discovered loose scraps of DNA in some pillbugs' cytoplasm responsible for changing genetic males into apparent females, and genetic females into bisexual members of pillbug populations.

The nerves in our body carry the memories that shaped the organization of our
nervous system to certain environmental circumstances. . . .
Joseph Campbell in *The Power of Myth*

*We accept with joy the seasons of nature. We honor them. We wouldn't
think of pulling at the tiny blades of grass in early spring to force their growth.
Neither would we chastise them for growing too slowly or wilting
with the first frost of autumn.*
Melody Beattie in *Journey to the Heart*

*H*ow does a thin blade of **grass** manage to push through a ce-
ment sidewalk? The stamina of grasses is a phenomenal wonder
that happens to be so common that we don't give it even a first
glance. Their roots zigzag every which way with a determination
to find moisture. Imagine being eaten, frozen, burned, drowned,
or dehydrated . . . and you keep on living anyway.

Not only do grasses survive under the most strenuous circumstances, they stay on their own schedule and go where they
want. Grasslands cover about a third of all habitable land in the
world.

Each blade of grass has its Angel that bends over it and whispers, "Grow, grow."
The Talmud

September 6

Of all spiders, **jumping spiders** (*Metaphidippus*) have the keenest vision, using their eight eyes to see forward with binocular strength, up, down, right, and left.

Even though they don't spin webs, they still make silk threads to use as safety lines as they leap from one position to another.

Swinging to a female's web, a male courts her by rhythmically swaying back and forth, enticing her with his strong hairy legs and shiny skin. His success depends on if he can get close enough to deposit his sperm before she eats him.

These engaging little animals, whose habit of cocking their heads to look at you gives them an almost human charm, stalk their prey like a cat and then jump on it explosively and without warning. Explosive it more or less literally is, by the way, for they jump by hydraulically pumping fluid into all eight legs simultaneously—a little like the way we (those of us who have them) erect our penises, but their "leg erections" are sudden rather than gradual.

Richard Dawkins in *Climbing Mount Improbable*

Don't get caught in the thick of thin things.
Earl Nightingale in *Earl Nightingale's Greatest Discovery*

The webs of **fall webworms** (*Hyphontria cunea*) are commonly seen on trees throughout the United States in the fall.

Distinct webs of fine silk are created by hundreds of webworms attached to the ends of branches of a single tree. If their tree should be disturbed, the caterpillars respond in unison with jerky but synchronized motions, making the tree look like it's shaking off a pest.

Eventually, the small caterpillars emerge as mature adults—white moths that fly at night meeting other night-flying moths to carry on the next generation of webworms.

> *Strangers in the night,*
> *exchanging glances,*
> *wond'ring in the night,*
> *What were the chances,*
> *we'd be sharing love,*
> *before the night was through?*
> "Strangers in the Night" by Charles Singleton,
> Eddie Snyder, and Bert Kaempfert

*B*efore the illegal selling of **house finches** (*Carpodacus mexicanus*) to bird dealers in New York City, the colorful little bird lived only in the west. In the 1940s, New York dealers released the captive house finches into the wild to get rid of evidence of their illegal activity. Since then, the birds have been spreading westward.

They are called *house* finches because of their ease in adapting to towns and suburbs, one of the traits that appealed to bird dealers. Their genus name is from the Greek meaning "fruit biter." The beak of the finch is made for cracking fruits and seeds with hard coverings. Their main food of weeds and thistles is common in city lots and neighborhood yards.

A rule of thumb says that, in birds such as the house finch, color variations occur in local populations, the darker plumage appearing in those that inhabit more humid areas. The naturalized eastern house finches do seem to be darker and, in addition, to have larger bills and shorter wings, tails and legs, and also less variation in their songs than the California race. When—and if—the two populations meet along some frontier in the West, it may be that there will be two distinct species.
Jake Page and Eugene S. Morton in *Lords of the Air*

Flocks of **American goldfinches** (*Carduelis tristis*) are commonly seen through the summer when other small birds have already paired off and are nesting. American goldfinches eat weed seeds such as thistles—but because thistles don't ripen until late summer, their nesting season is delayed so that a good supply of food will be available for the parents and their chicks. Also, the down from thistle is used in their nest construction.

After nesting, they return to flocks, often joining with other small birds such as redpolls and siskins to begin their migration south before the cold weather arrives.

The males, who are seasonally feathered in attractive yellow for breeding, lose their bright color in exchange for a more suitable plumage of camouflage brown.

> *[Some songbirds] have such dull plumage and so few visible marks of identification that only an expert armed with a battery of manuals can figure out what they might be, and there are [some] clad in so conflicting a patchwork of brilliant colors that a designer who tried to use such a scheme would be howled out of the showroom.*
> Ronald Orenstein in *Songbirds*

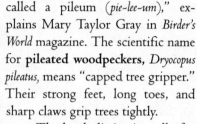

"*PILL-ee-ated* is what most people say, though purists will tell you it's a *PIE-lee-ated*, named for the top of the woodpecker's head, called a pileum (*pie-lee-um*)," explains Mary Taylor Gray in *Birder's World* magazine. The scientific name for **pileated woodpeckers,** *Dryocopus pileatus*, means "capped tree gripper." Their strong feet, long toes, and sharp claws grip trees tightly.

The loud, distinctive call of a pileated woodpecker is usually heard before the woodpecker is seen. Even though they have the basic eye-catching lines and colors of most woodpeckers—flashy red, black, and white—they manage to stay hidden, even in open urban areas.

Pileateds adjusted to losing their ancient habitat more readily than their cousin the ivory-billed woodpecker. Pileateds ventured beyond their familiar forests into areas that may not have been as protective, but provided food and opportunities to build nests.

The familiar life horizon has been outgrown; the old concepts,
ideals, and emotional patterns no longer fit; the time for
the passing of a threshold is at hand.
Joseph Campbell in *The Hero with a Thousand Faces*

*B*onding between **mallard** (*Anas platyrhynchos*) couples can last for the life of the pair, even among homosexual pairs. Female couples often remain together for life, either with or without raising offspring.

Researcher Bruce Bagemihl in *Biological Exuberance* describes male homosexual pairs consistently seeking the company of other males even when opposite-sex mates are available. "They maintain their homosexual bonds year after year (or re-pair with males after the death of a partner) in spite of persistent overtures from females. . . . There is also evidence that homosexual Mallard Ducks prefer each other's company and tend to congregate together: when large numbers of male pairs were brought together in captivity, for instance, they tended to form their own flocks and socialize with each other rather than with heterosexual birds."

The sexual enthusiasm typical of males may contribute to the prevalence of male homosexual behavior in humans and many other animals, which contrasts sharply with the relative rarity of female homosexuality.
John Alcock in *Animal Behavior*

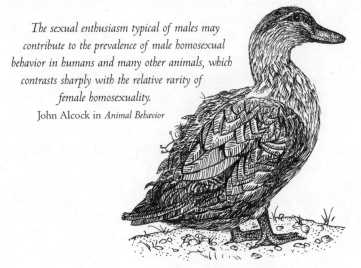

$\mathcal{T}$he sociability among insects ranges from the million-member colonies of ants to the solitary and private life of the **leaf-rolling caterpillar** (*Oecophylla*).

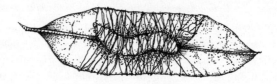

For shelter, these caterpillars roll themselves securely in leaves, fastening themselves with silk strands from edge to edge. The caterpillar moves its head from side to side, like a sideways sewing machine, threading the silk in and out of each side of the leaf. As the silk hardens in the air, it shrinks and pulls the leaf's edges close together. The leaf-rolling caterpillar stays inside its leaf-home by day, and leaves only at night, to look for food.

In September, many creatures experience the discomfort of being in between two seasons—the insistent tug of cold and hibernation after the high-energy days of sunlight and moisture. For humans, the discomfort of change is mostly ignored, rationalized away by the busyness of a new school or fiscal year. Shifting gears grates on many people who don't like change, but resistance only creates more discomfort.

One of the most difficult ideas for the human being to fully assimilate is that although we are social creatures, achievement is an individual and isolated affair.
Earl Nightingale in *Earl Nightingale's Greatest Discovery*

Killdeers (*Charadrius vociferus*) are masters at performing convincing charades to protect their chicks. By playing the "broken-wing ruse," killdeers lure predators away from their vulnerable chicks. The "injured" parent distracts the predator enough to lead it away from the nest and toward itself—easy prey—until the actor suddenly recovers.

The "bluff-brooding ploy" is another tactic killdeers use, pretending to sit on their eggs while actually the nest and eggs are being tended by the mate some distance away.

But another tactic—"confuse the big oaf"—is used when confronted with another type of danger: cows and horses. Killdeers, although known as shorebirds, are found in many inland areas including farms, fields, golf courses, and grazing pastures. When confronted with a cow or horse about to stomp on their nest, the broken-wing ruse would be in-effective—a cow simply wouldn't notice, or care—so instead, the killdeer launches into the face of danger, franti-cally flapping around its eyes and creating enough chaos to force the much larger animal to step aside, away from the ground-level nest.

> The bird lay low until the grazing quadruped was almost over the nest, then flew suddenly into its face with a great outcry, making the animal stagger back and circle the spot in confusion. After "a few dives and expostulations," the Killdeer returned quietly to its eggs, its objective accomplished.
>
> Alexander F. Skutch in *The Minds of Birds*

The very appropriate name for this common insect is more colorful in other languages. The Italian name for the grasshopper is cavalletta, *"little mare," while the Spanish call it* saltamontes, *"jump mountains." For some reason the Germans call it* die Heuschrecke, *"the terrible hay thing."*
Robert Hendrickson in *Ladybugs, Tiger Lilies and Wallflowers*

Grasshoppers (Tettigoniidae) have a catapult mechanism in their long hind legs that allows them to extend their legs faster than by muscle power alone, giving the impression that they can blast out of the grass as if from a launch pad. Hence their name *grasshopper.*

When male grasshoppers are ready to mate, they send out courtship chirps to attract females of their own species. The high-pitched signals are picked up by females that may or may not be willing enough to mate. When a male sees a female extending her antennae in response to his song, he changes his tune to another courtship song and approaches her. In some species, the male will begin hopping around her and may even jump on top of her to begin mating before she gives her permission. He persists until she either agrees or rejects him.

Men and women have trouble understanding each other because their bodies speak slightly different dialects of survival. Some of the words are the same, but the meanings vary, each gender has its own slang, and at times the grammar can be different.
Diane Ackerman in *A Natural History of Love*

*L*ocust (*Dissosteira*) is the Latin term for "grasshopper," and that's what a locust actually is—simply a short-horned grasshopper. They are loners, usually living in dry, open areas. Long periods of extremely dry weather force hordes of locusts to gather, and they reproduce to such an extent that overcrowding results. The wingless nymphs begin a migratory walk during which physical changes occur in their bodies, as if prompted for action, and their wings begin to grow extra long and strong.

Eventually this huge population takes to the air, consuming massive amounts of nourishment to maintain their energy as they migrate hundreds of miles, forming plagues of biblical fame.

When social animals are gathered together in groups, they become qualitatively different creatures from what they were when alone or in pairs. Single locusts are quiet, meditative, sessile things, but when locusts are added to other locusts, they become excited . . . and when there are enough of them packed shoulder to shoulder, they vibrate and hum with the energy of a jet liner and take off.

Lewis Thomas in *The Lives of a Cell*

The silk homes of **tent caterpillars** (*Malacosoma*) look like someone dropped a cloud onto a tree and it splattered all over the branches. Each tent is a communal web of caterpillars using the tree's branches as the foundation for their homes.

Newly hatched caterpillars gather at the forks and notches of branches and within a week begin to build their temporary housing by spinning fine strands of silk. As the caterpillars grow, so do the tents, sometimes engulfing the entire host tree. After six weeks or so of communal living, molting, and feeding, each individual caterpillar ventures out alone to find a place to build a cocoon in which it will change into a moth.

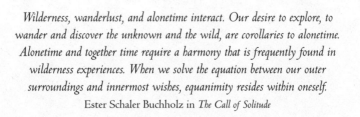

Adult moths emerge from the cocoons in the summer, flying off to begin mating and laying eggs.

Wilderness, wanderlust, and alonetime interact. Our desire to explore, to wander and discover the unknown and the wild, are corollaries to alonetime. Alonetime and together time require a harmony that is frequently found in wilderness experiences. When we solve the equation between our outer surroundings and innermost wishes, equanimity resides within oneself.

Ester Schaler Buchholz in *The Call of Solitude*

What happens to ducks in the winter when lakes and rivers freeze? A few die, but most find moving water that won't freeze. When their own territory thaws, they return.

In *The Lives of Birds*, Lester Short describes the dwindling population of **wood ducks** (*Aix sponsa*) on a lake in Maine. Local skunks had been eating the ducks' eggs, so nearby humans, wanting to be helpful, eliminated the skunks. But the duck population continued to dwindle and within two years, were completely gone.

In addition to eating duck eggs, skunks also eat snapping turtle eggs. Eliminating the skunks allowed the snapping turtles to multiply abundantly. When this huge population of turtles began foraging for food, the lake residents were open game. The turtles would lie in wait underwater until a duck passed over, yank it by the feet, drown it, and then eat it. Wood ducks are the snapping turtles' favorite food.

The human animal, too, is in the middle of a predatory chain. This idea ticks off a lot of people who, generally because of some religious or cultural bias, think we ought to be bosses of the animal kingdom. ("Kingdom": even that bit of taxonomic apparatus shows a human bias toward thinking in hierarchies.)
Gordon Grice in *The Red Hourglass: Lives of the Predators*

Female **wood ducks** nest in tree cavities and lay up to fifteen eggs. After about four weeks of incubation, the chicks hatch. Soon after hatching, they jump from their nest in response to their mother's call.

Imprinting occurs in a newly hatched duckling when it focuses on an object for ten minutes. Usually the object of attention is the mother duck, and the ducklings will follow her wherever she goes. Whoever the ducklings encounter first will be the one they stick with. Konrad Lorenz, in a now-famous study, showed that chicks would waddle after a substitute (himself) after hatching. Not only did they learn to recognize him, they cried when he wasn't close. Months later the males courted human beings.

Remarkably enough, he recognized the human mouth in an anatomically correct way as the orifice of ingestion and he was overjoyed if I opened my lips to him, uttering at the same time an adequate begging note. This must be considered an act of self-sacrifice on my part, since even I cannot pretend to like the taste of finely minced worms, generously mixed with jackdaw saliva.
Konrad Lorenz

*U*nlike many other woodpeckers in which the males and females look alike, male flickers have a distinctive mustache. When researchers painted a fake mustache on a female flicker, other females were attracted to her. Her mate didn't recognize her and began attacking her as he would a competitor.

Northern flickers (*Colaptes auratus*) are losing their habitat in some areas—not only from development, but from starlings, who have taken over the trees that flickers need for nesting and feeding. Flickers need the soft wood of rotting trees or bark. Their beaks are not as strong as other woodpeckers and can't pound into hard tree trunks.

At the Kennedy Space Center in 1995, the space shuttle *Discovery* was postponed because flickers were testing the soft brown of the fuel tank insulation and riddling it with holes. The foam had the same texture as rotting wood—a good source for insects. When one hole produced no insects, the flicker simply moved an inch or so and began to drill another hole, until the foam was dotted with hundreds of holes.

How we spend our days is, of course, how we spend our lives.
Annie Dillard in *An American Childhood*

Maybe goldenrod's being the flower that closes summer's shop is the real reason it bears the ill reputation it does; in fact the plant is innocent of the main charge brought against it.

Castle Freeman, Jr., in *Spring Snow*

Goldenrod (*Solidago*) gets the blame for most allergy problems because it blooms about the same time as the real culprit, ragweed. Goldenrod, however, is pollinated by insects, not airborne pollen. Also, goldenrod pollen is too heavy to drift in the air like other pollens.

The leaves from some goldenrods can be brewed for tea to relieve stomach cramps, colds, coughs, and fevers.

To understand the concept of medicine in the Native American way, one must redefine "medicine."... [It] is anything that improves one's connections to the Great Mystery to all life. This would include healing of mind, body, and of spirit. This medicine is also anything which brings personal power, strength, and understanding.

Jamie Sams and David Carson in *Medicine Cards*

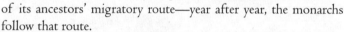

The migration of thousands of animals begins when autumn releases its heavy layer of cold air across the United States. Among the first wave of migrants are the **monarchs** (*Danaus plexippus*). Western monarchs travel to California, and those from the east spend the winter in Mexico. Each monarch, though it has never traveled before, has a map of its ancestors' migratory route—year after year, the monarchs follow that route.

Monarchs use the earth's magnetic field to guide them. Magnetite in their tissues detects the magnetic force, enabling them to travel many thousands of miles. If genes can pass along the "memory" of a migratory route from one generation of monarchs to the next, humans, with even more sophisticated wiring, could certainly inherit ancestral memories. Or at least some people have inherited a good sense of direction.

Monarch migration is listed with the International Union for the Conservation of Nature as the world's only "endangered phenomenon."

*If you find that you have been fighting your nomadic instincts . . . you are
cutting off that one set of instincts for which all the others may have
been made—your opportunity to move out into the world
and discover it in all its limitless glory and mystery.*
Wayne Dyer in *The Sky's the Limit*

Milkweeds (*Asclepias*) flourish everywhere. They are poisonous to most animals. A few, however, such as monarch butterflies and milkweed beetles, are immune to milkweed's poison—they even use the venomlike substance for their own protection. The name "milkweed" comes from the milky-white sap that contains the toxins.

Milkweed flowers are designed to capture insect pollinators. Even though monarchs land on milkweeds, they carry away no pollen, so other methods evolved for survival. Each blossom has five little packets of nectar; when an insect lands, its feet slip in between the flimsy landing surface, into a pollen-laden crevice. The pollen sticks to the insect's legs. When the insect visits the next flower, it slips again, this time losing the nectar and picking up new baggage.

Whether through bees by day or moths by night, the milkweed succeeded in engineering a pickup and delivery service for its pollen.

Flowers have no role in the life of their plant other than to exchange genes with another plant that has a different hand of genes.
Richard Dawkins in *Climbing Mount Improbable*

*F*lashy colors in the insect world are visual warnings to birds and other predators to stay away. The **monarch**'s bright colors advertise their bad taste to any animal looking for nutritious insect flesh. However, immature birds who have never tasted the poisonous monarch and can't resist the attractive red and black wings become sick from eating them. A blue jay will throw up within half an hour of eating a monarch, and will probably never repeat the experience.

The monarch's unpleasant taste is from consuming the poisons in the milkweed plants from the time they hatch. As larvae they gain an immunity from their host plant, and the molecules of poison remain potent in their tissues long after a monarch caterpillar has changed into a butterfly.

Some monarchs are known to eat dogbane, a nonpoisonous plant. These monarchs, even though they aren't toxic, are still protected from predators who don't know that a good-flavored monarch is available.

A vomited monarch does not fly off into the sunset.
John Alcock in *Animal Behavior*

Biology is destiny.
Sigmund Freud

𝒜 **monarch**'s transformation—from an egg to a caterpillar—to a pupa—to a fat body with little wings—to a flying work of art—happens millions of times every day as if it were the simplest thing in the universe to do.

I was always looking outside myself for strength and confidence, but it comes from within. It is there all the time.
Anna Freud

*H*undreds of North American wasp species range from smaller than a pinhead to longer than a horsefly, and from harmless to dangerous. Discovering new species has spurred creativity among those tasked with naming them. Wasp scientist Paul Marsh named these three wasps: *Verae peculya, Heerz tooya,* and *Heerz lukenatcha.*

Parasitic wasps, like the one shown here, *Microplitis croceipes,* use the bodies of caterpillars to lay their eggs. How do these wasps find the right caterpillar host amid the mass confusion of summertime activities? Not only can they smell the potential host and its droppings, they can detect signals in the air from the *plants* on which the host caterpillar is crawling. When a caterpillar begins chewing its meal, the plant responds by sending out signals. These signals are picked up by the female wasp, which then efficiently zooms in on her unsuspecting incubator-host.

> *Ninety-nine percent of the animals find their way by chemical trails laid over the surface, puffs of odor released into the air or water, and scents diffused out of little hidden glands and into the air downwind. Animals are masters of this chemical channel, where we are idiots.*
> Edward O. Wilson in *The Diversity of Life*

Norway rats (*Rattus norvegicus*) came to North America in the 1700s by boat from Asia. With five litters a year, up to ten babies in each litter, and the ability to start reproducing early, rats spread through the States rapidly. They can live in sewers as readily as basements or trees, and can climb, swim, run, crawl, and hide almost anywhere.

Play activity among young rats prepares them for their survival tactics used later in life. To let siblings know that it's playtime, "play signals" are given: a young rat will run, stop suddenly, flip over, and stay still—a sign of vulnerability that establishes its playful intent so siblings will join in.

Nothing in nature arises because it is fun, although much that we need to do ends up feeling so good that we're inspired to keep on doing it. . . . The most boisterous young animals of nature, among them pronghorn fawns, Norway rats, and human children, spend on play 20 percent of the calories not needed to simply keep them alive. . . . All costs considered, evolution would never have permitted its newcomers to be so frisky were friskiness not critical to an animal's growth.

Natalie Angier in *The Beauty of the Beastly*

What doesn't kill me makes me stronger.
Albert Camus

Norway rats will eat anything except things that have made them sick in the past. Poisoning rats, for this reason, is almost impossible. Strategies for avoidance have been perfected by generations of rats being subjected to poisons.

For hundreds of years, poisons were developed solely to eliminate rats. The rats, however, consistently became resistant to each new poison. Not only were the rats able to eat the poison with no ill effects, they developed "cautiousness" in trying new foods. This cautiousness of the survivors was passed along to the next generation, which became "ultracautious." Societies of rats were able to snub their collective noses at humans' backfired strategies.

The fact that they can take notice of what happens to other rats and transmit what they know to young rats in the next generation makes them formidable opponents indeed. If we do not concede that they have a "culture," then that must be because we have moved the goal posts and redefined what we mean by culture.
Marian Stamp Dawkins in *Through Our Eyes Only?*

September 28

Our deeds still travel with us from afar
And what we have been makes
us what we are.
George Eliot

Wood rats (*Neotoma*) are found almost everywhere in North America. They look like our brown Norway rats but their tails are hairier.

Also known as pack rats or trade rats, they collect food and building materials during their nightly wandering. An object will be hauled toward their home until a *better* object is found; they drop the first object, carry the better one . . . until an even better object is found, and so on. Hence, their common name *trade rat*. Campers often wake up to discover a twig has replaced a shiny fork, compliments of a pack rat.

The past few years have made us aware as we have never been before
of the depth of kinship among all living organisms . . . so all life is akin,
and our kinship is much closer than we had ever imagined.
George Wald in "The Search for Common Ground"
in *Zygon: Journal of Religion and Science* 11 (1966)

Rat snakes (*Elaphe*) are commonly found in swamps, woods, farms, and cities. Their colors and designs vary greatly, ranging from solid black to orange and yellow blotches. As their name suggests, they eat rats and other rodents (in addition to frogs, lizards, and birds).

Their tongues are sensory organs that they flick out to taste the air around them. Their ability to "taste" the scent of a rat makes them highly effective rodent controllers. Although they put on a convincing show of aggression by hissing, opening their mouths as if ready to strike, and shaking their ineffective tail, rat snakes are harmless to humans.

Like other snakes, they swallow their prey whole, going for long periods without eating as they digest this one, long-lasting meal. Some humans show this eating behavior while other animals, including humans, graze through the day, eating small portions. What works for one species won't work for another. The range in eating patterns among humans varies as greatly as in the animal kingdom.

It's great that we can run out for hamburgers, instead of running down a wild boar. It's nice to watch television, instead of chopping wood or fetching water. But the risks are enormous to people genetically built for the Stone Age.
Dean Hamer in *Living with Our Genes*

$\mathcal{D}$ark and mottled, **wolf spiders** (*Lycosa*), although common, are difficult to see among the leaves, dirt, and rubble where they live.

The female wolf spider is known for her devoted mothering skills, protecting her egg sacs by dragging them with her wherever she goes. As soon as the spiderlings are born, they cling to their mother's body and legs by hanging on to special hairs. They stay with her even as she hunts through the night. The spiderlings may jump off for a drink of water from time to time but always return to their mother until mature enough to live on their own.

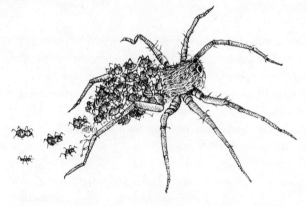

Male wolf spiders, however, only visit to mate, then leave permanently after mating.

A woman spins out a web of forevers, which she finds reassuring and cozy.
She tries to build an extended family in the community, give parties, do things
together as a couple. The man says he needs his space, doesn't understand
her mania for socializing, and doesn't want to feel tied
down, or that she's smothering him.
Diane Ackerman in *A Natural History of Love*

*R*ed-headed **woodpeckers** (*Melanerpes erythro-cephalus*) are creative investors. Through the year they store food in trees for the long winter months when acorns and nuts won't be available. They tuck food into holes and cracks in trees, finding different-sized openings to hold the various nuts and seeds. Months are devoted to poking, adjusting, angling, and covering their stashes with bits of bark and tiny twigs—until supplies are no longer available.

In the late summer, when grubs and other insects are plentiful they eat those, taking advantage of the abundance while it lasts, and only return to the hidden food when fresh supplies are gone. They defend their cache against other woodpeckers and birds through the winter until mating begins, when they move on to a nesting territory.

This assumption of a human monopoly on conscious thinking becomes more and more difficult to defend as we learn about the ingenuity of animals coping with problems in their normal lives.
Donald R. Griffin in *Animal Thinking*

What's the difference between **butterflies** and **moths**? Of the several differences, the most obvious is that moths fly at night. Also, the antennae of moths are slender or feathery at the tips, and butterflies' antennae are clubbed. Although both moths and butterflies use their antennae to detect odors, butterflies also have sense organs in their feet to smell and taste food. A butterfly will use its vision to locate nectar-producing flowers, but once it lands, it relies on its feet to find the pool of nectar.

To warm up, butterflies bask in the sun, but moths raise their body temperature by "shivering" their muscles.

A group of butterflies will gather around a puddle or wet area: this communal get-together is called a drinking club or *puddling* club and is usually all male. While drinking, the butterflies become so absorbed with their tasks that they can be approached easily without their noticing. Females, however, typically dart from flower to flower, looking for a suitable spot to lay their eggs.

It is the soul's duty to be loyal to its own desires.
It must abandon itself to its master passion.
Rebecca West

*I*mported by an amateur naturalist in
the mid 1800s to develop a better
silkworm for commercial
production, the **gypsy moth**
was thought to be of the
genus *Bombyx* but turned
out to be *Lymantria dis-
par*—"the destroyer"—
an apt name for these little
creatures that can destroy a forest.

   When one of the moths escaped from
his site in Massachusetts, the experimenter informed authorities,
but they chose to take no action. Within twelve years his neighborhood was covered with so many caterpillars that the streets and
sidewalks were slippery from all the gypsy moth larvae. Because
the moths had no natural predators in the United States, they
spread through the northeast, taking over their host trees as their
numbers increased.

   The tiny larvae were carried easily by wind; they could spin
silk thread to suspend themselves from leaves and sway back and
forth until they became airborne. By the 1970s the little moths had
denuded millions of acres of plants and trees.

*Mother Earth, lately called Gaia, is no more than the commonality
of organisms and the physical environment they maintain with each passing
moment, an environment that will destabilize and turn
lethal if the organisms are disturbed too much.*
Edward O. Wilson in *The Diversity of Life*

---

*A*ll butterflies and moths come from **caterpillars,** the immature stage that emerges from an egg. The word *caterpillar* started with the old French term *chatepelose,* meaning "hairy cat." The word transformed by combining "pill," meaning plunder and "cater," an old word meaning glutton. The term eventually evolved, as happens naturally with words, into caterpillar—greedy pillager—a fitting description of these eating machines. Caterpillars eat with a nonstop determination from the moment they hatch—even eating their own eggshell as they crawl out.

Caterpillars, after a certain growing period, stop being caterpillars and change from fat, wormlike creatures into furry winged flyers—with no more ability to stop the process than the earth could stop itself from turning.

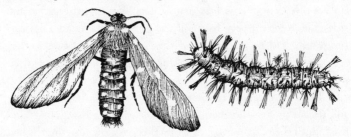

Because the nature of evolution is sloppy and unpredictable, thank God, we have butterflies with hairy wings, moths with silver spots, skippers with dancing feet . . . huge eyes, tiny eyes, fake eyes, goggle eyes—as if a bunch of artists were set free with clay and paint and told to go crazy.

Your work is to discover your work and then with
all your heart to give yourself to it.
Buddha

*L*eaf-rolling crickets (*Camptonotus carolinensis*) are active at night, hunting aphids and other small animals. Their exceptionally long antennae—twice the length of their body—are typical of night creatures. They use the sensitive antennae to feel their way around leaves and soil as they forage for food.

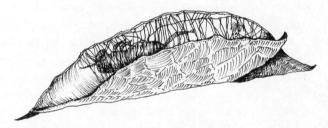

Before dawn, however, the cricket begins searching for a good-sized leaf, which it will use as a temporary home during the day. With its jaws, the leaf roller cuts slits in the leaf, to pull one leaf section toward itself with its feet. It then begins to sew itself inside using silk thread from its mouth, like a sewing machine, moving back and forth connecting the sides of the leaf.

With its long antennae coiled around its body, the leaf-rolling cricket remains motionless through the day, resting and regaining stamina for the active night to come.

Mother nature gives aloneness a high priority, viewing it differently than does American culture. For instance, nature built in a system that monitors sleep-wake cycles, called "circadian rhythms"—those internal clocks that help regulate our day and evening cycles, affecting many behaviors including sleeplessness and wakefulness. Sleep is nature's way of ensuring alonetime.

Ester Schaler Buchholz in *The Call of Solitude*

$\mathcal{U}$**gly nest caterpillars** (*Archips cerasivoranus*) spin dense webs, easily identified by the bits of black excrement clinging to the messy web. The larvae pupate in this clutter, emerging as orange moths between July and September.

The caterpillars living in these messy arrangements are yellowish green with shiny black heads—worthy of their common name, *ugly nest caterpillars.* They are harmless to their host plants, which are often rose bushes—a good balance, that one of the most beautiful of all plants provides housing for one of the ugliest of all insects.

Evolution, according to François Jacob, works "like a tinkerer who does not know exactly what he is going to produce but uses whatever he finds around him … to produce some kind of workable object." The relationship between the bushes and this ugly nest caterpillar works—both benefit from the other and most important, both survive.

One of the advantages of being disorderly is that one is
constantly making exciting discoveries.
A. A. Milne, as quoted in *Simple Abundance,*
by Sarah Ban Breathnach

*The Indians addressed all of life as a "thou"—the trees,
the stones, everything. You can address anything as a
"thou," and if you do it, you can feel that change in
your own psychology. The ego that sees a "thou" is
not the same ego that sees an "it."*
Joseph Campbell in *The Power of Myth*

A **century plant** (*Agave*) reaches maturity in ten to fifty years, not one hundred years as its name implies. A thick stalk emerges from the middle of the plant, growing, at times, two inches per day, sometimes growing taller than a telephone pole.

After blooming, the plant dies, losing its strength and toppling over from its own weight. Bulbils, small bulbs at the stem tops, fall and eventually grow into new plants. Century plants have an edible starchy heart, as big as a cabbage, with a hot flavor.

*Evidence now supports the vision of the
poet and the philosopher that plants are
living, breathing, communicating
creatures, endowed with personality
and the attributes of soul.*
Peter Tompkins and Christopher
Bird in *The Secret Life of Plants*

---

*O*ver 35,000 types of **spiders** have been classified, but tens of thousands more may still be discovered. About three thousand species live in the United States. Of those, only two are truly dangerous to humans: the black widow and brown recluse.

The range and variety of spiders are like no other animal on Earth: they live in cold or hot extremes; in sand or water; in attics or underground; they wander or hardly move at all; they are microscopic or as big as a fist; they look like ants or bird droppings; they can live for twenty years or die after completing a cycle of birth and mating. Males usually die after mating, and females usually die after giving birth.

The earliest fossil evidence of spiders came from New York in rocks from 380 million years ago. The fossil spider has the silk-spinning organ, a spinneret. This, with the silk-producing gland, is unique to spiders.

To what extent are emotional reactions wired in at birth?
I would say that neither humans nor animals are, of necessity, innately
wired to fear bears or eagles, although some animals and humans
may be wired to fear say spiders and snakes.
Antonio R. Damasio in *Descartes' Error*

October 9

Cobwebs are made by **tangled-web spiders.** Their haphazard appearance is deceiving—they are effectively designed to protect the weaver as well as capture food. The spider throws sticky globs of silk to capture prey with a toss equal to any major-league pitcher. When abandoned, the cobweb's tangle of threads and gobs picks up dust particles, usually in abundance in cellars and dark unused places where they're typically found.

Those unused, messy corner webs serve a handy purpose in emergencies: the silk can be put on wounds to stop bleeding. Pharmaceutical researchers at the University of Wyoming have found that spider silk can be used on cuts; the silk effectively resists bacteria and viruses. Some hospitals now use spider silk externally as well as *inside* the body to store drugs that need to be released slowly.

There she sits in full view in the center of her orb web, on a swatch of white silk. She may even bob up and down if you come too close. Perhaps she is relying on an ingrained dislike of spiders, to keep you from walking through her web and ruining the work of many hours.

John Farrand (editor) in *Familiar Insects and Spiders*

*C*ommon throughout the United States in fields and gardens, the **yellow and black argiopes** (*Argiope aurantia*) display bold and colorful designs on their bodies, unusual for spiders who are normally reclusive and avoid attracting attention. The yellow bands on the argiope, however, may be a way for it to keep predators away by masquerading as a wasp.

Typical of many spiders, argiopes wrap insects in protective silk to eat later.

Spider weaves the webs of fate for those who get caught in her web and become her dinner. This is similar to humans who get caught in the web of illusion in the physical world, and never see beyond the horizon into the other dimensions.

Jamie Sams and David Carson in *Medicine Cards*

*I*n the fall, the female **argiope** lays hundreds of eggs in grape-sized egg sacs protected by a strong silk cover. She attaches the egg case to a nearby leaf or to the edge of her web. The eggs hatch in the fall and the spiderlings scamper free, perfect miniatures of the parents, and begin weaving their own tiny webs.

Spiderlings who survive their first few days crawl into secure and protected spots, hidden through the winter until they emerge fully grown months later.

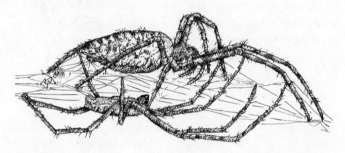

The new generation begins another cycle of mating. When a male argiope crawls on a female's web, he gently plucks the threads with his claws. His steady rhythm is different from the irregular movements of a caught insect. This lets the female know he's looking for a mate, so she won't respond to him as prey or predator.

The end of the story is not always happy for the male's mortal body, but his immortal genes are by now safely stowed away inside the female. The world is well supplied with spiders whose ancestors died after mating. The world is bereft of spiders whose would-be ancestors never mated in the first place.

Richard Dawkins in *Climbing Mount Improbable*

Whip scorpions (*Mastigoproctus*) are not true scorpions. They lack a venom-filled stinger, and have, in its place, a long tail with no apparent usefulness, at least not for defense. As a defense, however, when threatened they emit a powerful vinegar odor that repels most from approaching. Their common name is, in fact, *vinegaroon.*

Like true scorpions, vinegaroons hide during the day under logs and rocks and come out at night to forage, look for a mate, defend territory, or because they've been driven out by a larger force.

If survival needs are thwarted, rage, fear, and pain result. When they are met, we experience pleasure. . . . Neurobiologists often jokingly reduce limbic functions to the "four F's" of fighting, fleeing, feeding, and sex. From these basics, the more complex emotions of joy, rapture, grief, and empathy evolve with the appearance of the third level of the brain. . . .

Joan Borysenko in *A Woman's Book of Life*

Black widows (*Latrodectus mactans*) are one of the most dangerous spiders in the United States, to humans and other black widows.

During courtship the male approaches the female's web with caution, but if an agreeable series of vibrations occurs, he goes to her and binds her loosely with silk. After he transfers his sperm to her, she breaks the bonds and he leaves. If his exit isn't fast enough, she eats him. Hence her name.

Babies develop inside round silk egg cases and within a few weeks they tear the sacs and crawl out. They race toward protection—from insects, other spiders, their mother, and their siblings, all of whom would eat the spiderlings if given the opportunity. Grinding the tiny eggs in the silk egg sacs produces deadly toxins—some Native Americans used to smear the crushed eggs on arrowheads.

No explanation for the female black widow's unpredictable response has held up for long. Sometimes she eats the male without first copulating; sometimes she snags him as he withdraws his palp from her genital pore; sometimes he leaves unharmed after mating . . . Recently fed virgin females sometimes eat males.
Gordon Grice in *The Red Hourglass: Lives of the Predators*

---

*Walk down a lane overhung with trees in the never-never land of autumn, and
you will forget about time and death, lost in the sheer delicious spill of color.
Adam and Eve concealed their nakedness with leaves, remember?
Leaves have always hidden our awkward secrets.*
Diane Ackerman in *A Natural History of the Senses*

*F*all **leaves** don't actually *change* color; they *expose* color that was
already there. The green in leaves is from
chlorophyll, which breaks down when temperatures drop. The reds and
yellows (from carotene in the
leaves) are then uncovered, giving
fall leaves their bright colors.
But where does the green
go? The chlorophyll
and other minerals
return to the tree.

Flowers get all the
credit for being colorful
and sexy, as if leaves were just an afterthought. But not so! Leaves
are the heart and soul of a plant, literally drawing in life from the
resources of the universe: earth, air, and water.

Wag the world how it will, Leaves will be green in spring.
Herman Melville in "Malvern Hill"

"You have the greatest brain in the world, and I have the most beautiful body; so we ought to produce the most perfect child," wrote a lady in Zurich to George Bernard Shaw. He responded, "What if the child inherits my body and your brains?"

Killer bees (*Apis mellifera scutellata*) were created in the 1950s by a geneticist in South America to improve honey production by mating European honeybees with African honeybees. However, the mating resulted in a fiery-tempered bee, now known as a killer.

Basically, killer bees look like honeybees. They are slightly smaller and have shorter tongues and forewings. But their behavior is much more aggressive and erratic than honeybees, and they are nervous enough to attack with no provocation. The sting of a killer bee is no worse than that of a honeybee, but several thousand tiny doses of their venom can be fatal. When a bee is slapped or swatted, an alarm scent is released, a clear signal to the bee's gang to swarm to the rescue.

The reason for our success as a species is that we have made the most of our genes. We must not surrender to our harmful impulses, such as aggression, but rather channel them to our advantage—and for this, knowledge is the key.
Dean Hamer in *Living with Our Genes*

Bats forage for food when night skies are relatively traffic-free, using sonar to navigate through the dark. Their high-pitched sounds bounce off nearby objects and "echo" back, giving the bats exact positions of their prey. Bats also listen for the calls of animals, such as frogs—even distinguishing between poisonous and nonpoisonous frogs.

Bats are the only mammals to truly fly. (Flying squirrels actually glide.) Given their unique nature as flying mammals, bats are in a scientific group of mammals all their own: *Chiroptera,* which means "hand wing." Looking at their skeleton makes it easy to see the "hands" that give support to the wings.

Their gentle and beautiful faces reflect a range of variations found nowhere else within a mammal species. In China, bats represent the ingredients for happiness: health, longevity, and peace of mind. The Chinese character for bat, *fu,* is also the word for good luck.

Bats are feared only to the extent they are misunderstood.
Merlin D. Tuttle in *America's Neighborhood Bats*

Bats are known as insect
eaters, but many species eat
fruit, pollen, and nectar.
The various shapes of bat
faces, some with excep-
tionally long snouts,
help nectar-feeding bats
reach into plants that
have long, tubular
openings.

Some bats carry fruit
away to be eaten later. The
juice is extracted and the
seeds are spat out in a pellet, ensuring seed dispersal and increasing the chances of survival of the fruit species.

Feeding methods of bats vary, particularly the flower feeders,
but whether the bat lands on top of a stalk and works its snout
into the flower, or takes quick sips of nectar from the air, the bat
probably will fly away with pollen on its head. As the bat moves
from flower to flower, pollination occurs much the same way as
accomplished by insects and hummingbirds. The plants that bats
visit for food typically are night-blooming, on stalks, or emit a
strong aroma to attract the bats or other night-pollinating animals.

Respect the common things. They are common because they survived.
John C. Gifford in *Living by the Land*

*L*ittle **brown bats** (*Myotis lucifugus*) are probably the most abundant bats in North America; the ones we're most likely to see in our neighborhoods. Near streetlights that attract insects, they zigzag crazily through the summer sky, consuming hundreds of pounds of flying insects each night.

In late summer, little browns prepare to hibernate, and some will travel a thousand miles to their chosen cave, where they remain for six to eight months.

During hibernation, a bat's heart rate slows from 180 beats per minute to *three* per minute. Its respiration slows from eight breaths per second to eight per minute. Hibernating bats should never be awakened before they are ready: the process of returning to an awake state uses almost all their stored energy and they can die from the unnatural and unexpected shock. Transition from asleep to awake is as shocking for some humans, who need a gradual introduction to the day before adjusting to consciousness.

Ever since I can remember, clear back to childhood, my process on waking has felt more like some interior ancient re-enactment of the whole human drama, going back to protozoic times, rising through the slime, struggling up from the sea to reach land, crawling inch by inch over the dry terrain, and then, millions of eons later, by performing a miracle of will and coordination, rising to stand and then move forward on only two legs!

Dan Wakefield in *Creating from the Spirit*

If some bats had wingspans of four meters and enjoyed humans for dinner, I imagine that we would have evolved the capacity to detect these hunters in the dark.
John Alcock in *Animal Behavior*

Pallid bats (*Antrozous pallidus*) stay hidden during the day in eaves of buildings and crevices in rocks. Colonies of pallid bats are relatively small, only a dozen to one hundred or so members. They are easy to recognize by their large ears, which are nearly half as long as their entire body.

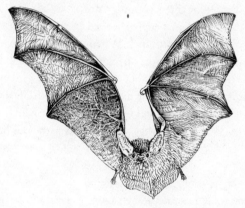

Mating begins in October, but the pups, typically twins, aren't born until the following June. Young bats don't learn to fly until they are about five or six weeks old.

Flying seems formidable to us mainly because we are large animals. . . . If you are a very small animal, the conquest of the air is no problem. When you are very small, the harder challenge may be to stay on the ground.
Richard Dawkins in *Climbing Mount Improbable*

In three words, I can sum up everything I've learned about life. It goes on.
Robert Frost

*F*or their size, **bats**
are the longest-lived
and slowest-reproducing
mammals on Earth. Some
bats live more than thirty years.
On average, females give birth only once
a year.

Young bats play by swooping after
each other, developing maneuvers needed later to capture insects.
Bats never collide with each other. When you see bats fly through
the night sky with their mouths open, it is simply to catch food on
the fly. They're not fast flyers, but they can maneuver better than
hummingbirds to position their mouths in the path of an insect.

Humans' fear that bats will try to fly into our hair at night is
simply a myth. Why would a bat want to mess with your hair, anyway?

*Though small in stature, the bat is a powerful symbol. Its medicine is
strong and can even be traumatic. It is a nocturnal animal, and the night was
often considered the home of fears. . . . Most people fear transitions, holding onto
a "better the devil you know than the one you don't" kind of attitude. If a bat
has flown into your life, then it is time to face your fears and prepare for
change. You are being challenged to let go of the old and create the new.*
Ted Andrews in *Animal-Speak*

I would like to learn, or remember, how to live.
Annie Dillard in *An American Childhood*

*P*regnant **free-tailed bats** (*Tadarida*) leave their mates every year in Mexico to fly hundreds of miles into the United States. They look for caves in areas where plenty of insects live. But since there are so few available caves in North America, millions of bats crowd into the few available ones to perform their nursing requirements. At night, they leave their pups in the cave to hunt for food.

Predators, such as screech owls, sometimes wait near the roosts for the bats to emerge. Just before dark and just after dawn, hawks position themselves to spot bats coming and going. When (and if) she returns to her cave after a night of foraging, each mother bat miraculously finds her own baby through calls; exchanging squeaks, a mother and her offspring will navigate toward each other until finally the pup presses itself into her armpit, where nipples provide milk.

Trust that reservoir of animal instincts you have kept deeply guarded with you, and rely more on your natural human abilities than on all the cultural rules for behavior that you have learned.
Wayne Dyer in *The Sky's the Limit*

Butterflies use coloring as a warning against predators, but **moths,** who are generally camouflaged by darkness, use other tactics to protect themselves, more suited for night flying. The large "eyes" on the inside of some moths' wings give the impression, even if for just a moment, of an owl or other threatening bird. The message received by the attacker creates enough confusion to give the moth a second to escape. Who wouldn't be startled when faced with an unexpected pair of wide-open eyes in a dark place?

Moths also flap their wings wildly while rocking from side to side as another way to distract an approaching bird. This creates an image that the predator has a larger and crazier opponent to contend with, and it might hesitate for a moment before attacking.

Sensing "wrong" chemicals, unfamiliar vibrations, strange noises, and unidentifiable shapes are all triggers that are heeded among animals for survival.

Your inner biology will see you through virtually any circumstance with your safety and health intact, if only you will permit it to function. The essence of becoming a good animal is learning to trust your body. . . .
Wayne Dyer in *The Sky's the Limit*

$\int$**piders** manufacture several types of silk; some threads are sticky enough to snare a passing insect, strong enough to hold it, and long enough to wrap and store it for a later meal. Some silk strands aren't sticky at all so the spider won't get stuck on them herself. Some strands are whitish as a warning to birds. Some strands are used to protect egg sacs. All these are made by spinnerets, nozzles at the rear end of the spider's abdomen.

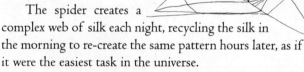

The spider creates a complex web of silk each night, recycling the silk in the morning to re-create the same pattern hours later, as if it were the easiest task in the universe.

Ignoring a natural longing to weave, sew, cross-stitch, or string threads together is denying our nature—as much a part of some people as spinning a web is for spiders.

> *The spider is the master weaver. To the Native Americans*
> *Grandmother Spider kept and taught the mysteries of the past and how*
> *they were affecting the future. Spider reminds us to awaken*
> *our own sensibilities to be more creative in life.*
> Ted Andrews in *Animal-Speak*

When people have nightmares, it's principally because they have been repressing the biology and it comes up with a vengeance. . . . Nature becomes feared if it has been suppressed long enough and you are out of accord with it. . . .
Joseph Campbell in *An Open Life*

Burrowing owls (*Athene cunicularia*) are nonconformists by owl standards. Not only are they much smaller than most owls, they build their nests in underground burrows lined with grasses and leaf debris. They carry clumps of horse manure and pack it around the entrance of the nest, perhaps as an added camouflage or as a way to waterproof the burrow. Most other owls simply build large nests high in trees or take over another bird's nest.

Most owls are also nocturnal; although burrowing owls are active at night, they also conduct some chores like gathering food during the day—perhaps certain prey are more accessible by day. Whatever works, works. Animals care about survival, not about following rules.

Why should we be in such desperate haste to succeed, and in such desperate enterprises? If a man does not keep pace with his companions, perhaps it is because he hears a different drummer. Let him step to the music which he hears, however measured or far away.
Henry David Thoreau in *Walden*

Witch hazel (*Hamamelis*) is a scraggly cluster of yellow flowers that blooms in the fall and winter along streams and woods.

When the blossoms fall, they are replaced by seed capsules that stay on the branches for at least a year—until they burst open and shoot four seeds into the air with a powerful blast that carries them twenty feet or more.

Witch hazel sold in stores as a common antiseptic is made from the bark. It has been used by Native Americans for centuries to treat backaches, tumors, and ulcers.

Cherokees made tea from the leaves and bark to relieve colds and sore throats. Crushed leaves were rubbed over scratches and sores to soothe inflammation.

Witch hazel is used by those who put themselves under pressure by trying to live up to the expectations of others.
Anne McIntyre in *Flower Power*

Often seen rocking sideways from its perch high in a tree, an **owl** locates a small animal moving below—maybe a mouse rustling leaves—through sound, rather than smell or vision. Everything about owls is made for receiving sound: their disklike faces funnel noise to ears that are placed unevenly on the sides of their head. This pinpoints their prey by receiving sound waves of varying lengths.

Owls swoop up their prey—rats, mice, lizards, small birds, frogs, cats, rabbits—then, from their eating perch, swallow it whole. But owls can't digest the fur, bones, and teeth. After eight hours or so, once or twice a day, depending on the owl, they regurgitate the material—known as "casting the pellet"—the equivalent of a cat hurling a hairball.

There are some who cannot resist picking up an owl pellet with its bits of bone,
fur, teeth, and feathers and taking it on as a puzzle. Each pellet is a mystery,
and behind it is the drama of a predator lurking in the night.
Bernd Heinrich in *One Man's Owl*

I love to think of nature as an unlimited broadcasting station, through which God speaks to us every hour, if we will only tune in.
George Washington Carver

$\int$creech owls (*Otus asio*) are named for their call, but they actually sound like witches wailing on Halloween night—haunting, trilling, and surreal. People are usually surprised when they discover the source of the far-reaching sound—a little pipsqueak, not much larger than a robin and much smaller than their call suggests.

Screech owls are often mistaken for immature great horned owls because of their body shape and tufts. But screech owl chicks are, like most owl chicks, cartoonlike fluffy balls of down with eyes and feet. Their distinguishing characteristics become apparent by the time they leave the nest.

Every human being carries with him from his cradle to his grave certain physical marks which do not change their character. . . . These marks are his signature, his physiological autograph. . . . There is no duplicate of it among the swarming populations of the globe.
Mark Twain in *Pudd'nhead Wilson*

You are a child of the universe no less than the trees and the stars;
you have a right to be here. And whether or not it is clear to you, no doubt
the universe is unfolding as it should.
Max Ehrmann

Maples (*Acer*) are traditionally a symbol of balance because they maintain their strength and identity while drastically changing through the seasons.

Papery, double-winged fruits of the maple, called "keys," fall through the air like miniature helicopters. They land in leaf litter and soil to become food for rabbits, birds, squirrels—or grow into the next generation of maples.

What we want in practice is to understand the nature of our lives,
and this does not demand a particular experience but a
quality of awareness that excludes nothing.
Sharon Salzberg in *A Heart as Wide as the World*

Barred owls (*Strix varia*) are notorious night stalkers, hunting for rats, mice, snakes, and other nocturnal animals.

"The early bird catches the worm," may be true for wrens and robins, but what about the barred owl, who doesn't care about worms anyway? A sleep expert at Stanford Medical School has linked internal clocks to a mutation in a chromosome 4 gene. In humans, a particular variant of the gene was found in nine out of ten early risers, while another variant of the same gene was found in "night owls."

A human who has the internal clock of this owl could never fully adjust to the standard eight to five schedule of the majority of humans. It's possible for some to adjust their sleeping schedule with light therapy and/or drugs; however, their basic nature, on a cellular level, remains that of a night creature. A tension will stay with them, like a pulled rubber band just waiting to snap back.

Imposing punishments and demanding that the child wake up on
time at any price usually only serves to exacerbate the problem and divert it to
psychiatric treatment with its concomitant stigma, from which
it is almost impossible to escape later in life.
Peretz Lavie in *The Enchanted World of Sleep*

About thirty species of **tarantulas** (Theraphosidae) live in North America. Their reputation as dangerous spiders is unfounded. They are actually less dangerous than bees or wasps. They do, however, have a nonvenomous defense system. When disturbed, they scrape off hairs from their abdomen using their strong legs. Lighter than air, these hairs float into the eyes and skin of predators. Barbs on the hairs inflame and irritate on contact.

Strictly nocturnal, tarantulas hunt by touch. During the day they stay hidden, safe in their dark burrows from day-hunting predators.

Like other spiders, their biological clock isn't a specific organ that can be reset like a watch. Rather, the timing mechanism, part of humans' biology, too, is dispersed through every cell of the body. Asking a night person to go to bed at 10:00 P.M. is as unnatural as expecting a tarantula to begin hunting at noon.

People whose sleeping hours have been completely opposite to those around them from an early age, and whose efforts to change this situation have been doomed to failure, are in a permanent state of frustration.

Peretz Lavie in *The Enchanted World of Sleep*

The fat caterpillar shown here is the immature stage of one of the most beautiful moths in North America. Most moths, compared with butterflies, are small and dull. But the **luna moth** (*Actias luna*) is large, colorful, powerful, and graceful. Two sets of bizarre owl eyes under feathery antennae, long ribbony trails dangling from behind green wings, and a furry bright white body are enough to catch anybody's attention. The luna moth lives for only three days: days filled with learning to fly, getting a mate, having sex, finding a host plant, and laying eggs—adults don't even have time to eat. With so much to accomplish in three days, they use a strategy that wastes no time: scare tactic.

A bird responds to the *symbol* of an owl's eyes in the same way a human reacts to a "beware of bad dog" sign even though no dog is visible. We see what we need to see to survive, whether by learned behavior or perception.

There's an uncanny feeling when a darkened doorway becomes a roomful of eyes and every shadow seems to grow a face. That fear, left over from some ancient instincts, is with us every day in an attenuated form.
James Elkins in *The Object Stares Back*

As their name implies, **evening grosbeaks** (*Hesperiphona vespertina*) have large and strong beaks used for cracking hard seeds such as those from sunflowers. Their beaks are yellow for most of the year, but blue-green in the spring. The color change is from losing the yellow outer coating of the bill to reveal the spring color underneath.

Like many songbirds, evening grosbeaks are migratory and display nocturnal restlessness prior to their spring and fall journeys. But, unlike the migratory habits of other songbirds, who travel between the north and south, evening grosbeaks travel irregularly, often from northwest to southeast. Each year some grosbeaks expand their range, traveling farther in all directions. Some linger through winter at sites where food is abundant, and some have become common dedicated backyard bird feeder visitors in the winter.

. . . Fall is a Time when shifts occur signaling that your future will be different from the past. Your main focus during this time is to acknowledge that a change is actually happening and you do what you can to prepare.
Carol L. McClelland in *The Seasons of Change*

*I*nside the fleshy pads of the **prickly pear cactus** (*Opuntia*) is a strong network of fibers that gives the plant its shape and holds it upright.

Sharp spines on the outside protect the meaty pads from predation, but a few animals manage to eat the fruit, or remove the nectar, and some even nest between the spikes.

The cochineal insect (*Dactylopius coccus*) feeds on the prickly pear cactus and would be unremarkable except that the females are collected by humans to make red dyes. These insects are tiny, scaly, and look like mealybugs. The females are gathered by Native Americans and many other cultures around the world, then dried and processed, either in boiling water or dry heat, depending on the crimson desired.

Gaia hypothesis perceives the earth as an infinitely complex living and evolving entity. . . . Gaia was the Greek goddess of the earth who created the universe and gave birth to the race of gods and the first human beings.

Anne McIntyre in *Flower Power*

*The chickadee is the top salesman of the
avian crowd—energetic, enthusiastic and optimistic.*
Al Batt in *Birds & Blooms* magazine

Black-capped chickadees (*Parus atri-capillus*) are little social migrants, traveling in bands each fall and mixing with several other species such as warblers, titmice, brown creepers, nuthatches, kinglets, and even woodpeckers. The chickadees stake out the best feeding areas, making the rounds of neighborhood bird feeders and often showing up in below-freezing weather.

Not only do the chickadees locate the best feeding spots for their own species and their traveling companions, they act as sentries when predators approach, by letting out a distinctive warning call. Chickadees spend a lot of time storing seeds in bark, crevices, and holes—and will remember the location of each cache when food supplies are low.

*Migratory birds often select their territories early in spring before vegetation is
well grown and productivity has approached its maximum, as it should do
weeks or months later when nestlings will need much nourishment.
A realistic forecast must be based on individual experience or racial memory
encoded in the bird's genes. Again, we do not know how the prospecting
female assesses her breeding territory, but her choice appears to
involve complex mental activity, including foresight.*
Alexander F. Skutch in *The Minds of Birds*

$\mathcal{M}$any wasps hibernate through the winter in logs or abandoned crevices in trees and stumps. Thousands of these are species of **ichneuman wasps** (Ichneumonidae), ranging from gnat-sized to longer than a hornet. Their long "stinger" is actually an ovipositor, an egg-laying organ incapable of harming anything.

Ichneuman wasps are also called tracker wasps because females track down the larvae of pigeon horntails (*Tremex*), another type of wasp. Horntails lay eggs in the bark of trees or in old logs. With her supremely sensitive antennae, a tracker wasp can detect vibrations of the horntail larvae under bark. Landing on the wood directly above the horntail larva, she bores through to lay *her* egg on the other wasp's offspring.

The drama continues, however, when yet *another* female wasp, a *fake* tracker wasp (*Pseudorhyssa*), comes along to use the ready-made hole to lay *her* egg on top of the previously laid egg. And there they stay through the winter.

The larval stages of all these species *may* develop to adulthood, but probably at least one will die. (Shown at top from left: tracker, horntail, and fake tracker wasps.)

People are always blaming their circumstances for what they are.
I don't believe in circumstances. The people who get on in this world are the
people who get up and look for the circumstances they want
and if they can't find them, they make them.
George Bernard Shaw

*B*ulging red eyes, red spots, and red veins distinguish the **box elder** (Leptocoria) from other common leaf-crawling insects.

As their name suggests, these insects use box elders as their host plant when available. They lay their eggs in the bark, and both the nymphs and adults feed on the plant juices. Adult female and nymph are shown here.

Swarms of females gather on tree trunks and around buildings in the fall looking for a place to spend the winter. They often let themselves into houses in search of a safe winter home in urban areas where trees and plants are not available. The ones who don't find a spot to spend the winter, die.

This is an absolute necessity for anybody today. You must have a room, or a certain hour or so a day. . . . This is a place where you can simply experience and bring forth what you are and what you might be. This is the place of creative incubation. At first you may find that nothing happens there. But if you have a sacred place and use it, something eventually will happen.
Joseph Campbell in *The Power of Myth*

The **American chestnut tree** (*Castanea dentata*), once valuable for its wood and food, was a dominant tree in U.S. forests until a fungus (*Cryphonectria parasitica*) was brought into New York harbor in the early 1900s. Most of the chestnut trees were destroyed within a short time. Botanists and naturalists were baffled, not only by what caused the mass destruction, but also how it spread so quickly.

Careful investigation showed that spores of the parasite had thin sticky threads that stuck to the feet and fur of mammals and birds—as many as seven thousand were counted on the foot of one woodpecker.

Of the few chestnut trees that survived, none had viable fruit, and any new sprouts were killed within five years of their emergence.

The tree does not end at its skin but exists also in the rain that falls downwind,
many miles from the forest. In the seed exists the acorn, the oak, and the shade.
The tree is also the fungi that live at its base, the bird that lives on its seed.
Stephen Harrod Buhner in *Sacred Plant Medicine*

*A single gentle rain makes the grass many shades greener. So our
prospects brighten on the influx of better thoughts.*
Henry David Thoreau

*C*rab **grass** (*Digitaria san-
guinalis*) is also called crow's
foot grass, pigeon grass, or finger
grass; the last term is most descriptive of
its fingers stretching upward. Its scientific
name means "cheerfully optimistic fingers." Crab
grass has every right to joyfully spread
itself over yards and fields—
what other plant can endure getting stomped on,
grazed over, mowed down, pulled out, played on,
and snowed under? Crab grass is as predictable
and dependable as summer heat.

*Nobody knows yet where the grass plant conceals a clock,
a weather station, and a communications network.
Yet it opens its flowers as though it possessed all of these.*
Lorus and Margery Milne in *Because of a Flower*

*£*arwigs (*Forficula*) are common and abundant in backyards, fields, and woods. We don't see them as much as we see ants, bees, or flies because earwigs are nocturnal, and they stay hidden under leaf debris or underground most of the day.

The female's protective nature is as gentle and dedicated as Lassie's or Mrs. Cleaver's, but for some reason, earwigs don't get as much credit for excellence in motherhood.

The female earwig constructs a safe burrow under rocks for her eggs, which she guards without leaving, even to eat, until after the eggs have hatched. She then forages for food, returning to the nest to feed her offspring. After a few days she takes them out to teach them how to hunt and how to protect themselves from danger. Each night they return to the burrow, guided by a trail of scent left by glands in the earwigs' feet.

Perhaps we don't hear the whispers of authentic longing because we don't want to hear. If we hear, we might have to acknowledge, even respond.
Sarah Ban Breathnach in *Simple Abundance*

*E*ven though **rove beetles** (*Ontholestes cingulatus*) are similar in appearance to earwigs, they differ greatly in behavior. After mating, male earwigs move on, having no more contact with the female or their offspring. A rove beetle, however, will guard his mate against potential rivals, defending her (and her stored sperm) to ensure his genetic future.

But if a stronger, larger, or faster male defeats the defender, the female will mate with the victor, using his sperm to replace or dilute the loser's.

> *Listen, People, to what I'm telling you.*
> *Keep away from Runaround Sue.*
> *She likes to travel around. Yeah.*
> *She'll love you, then she'll put you down.*
> *She likes to go out with other guys.*
> *Keep away from Runaround Sue.*

"Runaround Sue," by Dion DiMucci and Ernest Maresca

Adornment is never anything except a reflection of the heart.
Coco Chanel

The first **starlings** (*Sturnus vulgaris*) in the United States were released by Eugene Scheifflin in the late 1800s in New York's Central Park as part of a plan to import all the birds mentioned in Shakespeare's plays. Starlings now live in fifty states in almost every habitat.

They live in great flocks but keep discrete distances individually. Aggressive and opportunistic by nature, they protect territory—even a few inches of telephone wire—by sidling toward an invader and puffing out their wings to look threatening.

In the winter, the plumage of starlings is speckled with white, but in the spring it is a bold, iridescent purplish black. For most birds, feathers change by replacement (molting), but for starlings, the white tips of their feathers wear off. After the white wears off, the feathers stop wearing out, because a black pigment, *melanin,* makes them resistant to abrasion.

Beware of any activity that requires the purchase of new clothes.
Henry David Thoreau

We do not live in a Nuclear Age or an Information Age.
We do not live in a Post-Industrial Age, a Post—Cold War Age, or a Post-
Modern Age. We do not live in an Age of Anxiety or even a New Age.
We live in an Age of Flowering Plants and an Age of Beetles.
Sue Hubbell in *Broadsides from the Other Orders*

The **ground beetle** (*Calosoma scrutator*) is also known as the caterpillar hunter for its ability to track down larvae and worms, even climbing trees to follow a meal.

Adult ground beetles are shiny blackish purple, so they're easy to spot in fields, gardens, and woods as they prowl around hunting. Their larvae, however, hunt at night, needing the protection of darkness from their daytime predators such as birds.

In the fall, when food sources are scarce and temperatures drop, adults hibernate under the soil. In the spring, emerging from their winter dormancy, the search for mates begins with males approaching females. But females are not always receptive—a choosy female will release a potent liquid to signal a male that she's not interested.

Females spray unwanted suitors; a male covered with the repellant
attempts to clean his body with his mouthparts and then collapses. He remains
in a coma for several hours before reviving.
John Alcock in *Animal Behavior*

*F*ossils of **ginkgo** leaves (*Ginkgo biloba*) indicate that the tree has been around for more than 200 million years—its design has hardly changed at all, typical (although uncommon) of wildlife that finds a successful path through evolution.

Ginkgoes are related to evergreen trees, but instead of needles, they have distinctive fanlike leaves. Their resistance to insects, diseases, and pollution has allowed them to survive while other trees became extinct. However, the trees were almost destroyed in Asia by humans about A.D. 850. But Buddhist monks in Korea safeguarded some saplings in their monasteries to save them from extinction. Their efforts now provide us with the important herb that millions of people rely on for health.

Everything in nature has a purpose. No matter how odd it appears or how strange it behaves, there is some purpose. We may not understand it all, but how often do we understand the behaviors of those around us? . . . In our rationalistic society, it becomes difficult not to question the value of some plants, animals, and their interrelationships. We need to ask ourselves whether we need to justify the existence of a plant or animal anymore than the existence of people.
Ted Andrews in *Animal-Speak*

Let us train our minds to desire what the situation demands.
Seneca

The Spanish word for cockroach is *cucaracha*, meaning "contemptible little caterpillar." Everything about them makes humans feel uncomfortable: their legs are covered with hairs (which they use for tasting); they have long, probing antennae; and their shiny brown bodies are slick with a smelly oil that allows them to slip through tight spaces.

Cockroaches eat almost anything and live almost anywhere.

They can live three months without food and one month without water. They can even live for a while without their heads.

The **American cockroach** (*Periplaneta americana*) and the **German cockroach** (*Blatta germanica*), shown here, are two of the most familiar of the dozens of species that live in North America.

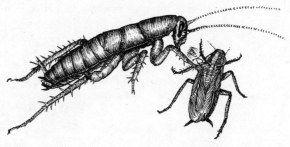

These two pest species have fared so successfully in their strategy of taking up residence with humans that they no longer have an independent existence or any representatives of their own kind in the wild. Whenever scientists in the field thought they'd stumbled on a free-ranging American or German cockroach, they always found a house somewhere nearby.
Natalie Angier in *The Beauty of the Beastly*

Cockroaches have changed little over the aeons. Like the designers of Volkswagen Beetles, they have stuck with what appears to be a winning formula, to which they've added countless refinements over time. The result of all this fine-tuning? An inconspicuous but well-equipped creature with alien features and abilities far beyond our own.
David George Gordon in *The Compleat Cockroach*

Sophisticated body parts on the **cockroach** have allowed it to survive nearly 400 million years of changing environments. Maxillary palps, two small appendages on each side of the mouth, are covered with thousands of tiny taste hairs. By tasting their food *before* eating it, they can avoid many poisons, many specifically created for them.

A female cockroach, having successfully avoided fatal poisons, matures to lay eggs in a protective little case called an *ootheca*, often found empty behind bookcases, in cabinets, and dark corners. One female can produce four to fifteen oothecas, each with two rows of about a dozen eggs. All newborns are born wingless but immediately begin looking for their own place near food and water. Shown here is a female about to release an ootheca.

Life is always attempting to move us in the direction of our own evolution and development . . . every experience and event of our lives is part of that process.
Shakti Gawain in *Creating True Prosperity*

*I've learned details about cockroach biology that make me want to
salute them . . . the great cockroach saga. It is the story of persistence and
resistance, of sensitivity and ceaseless change.*
Natalie Angier in *The Beauty of the Beastly*

When **cockroaches** are born they are wingless, white, and lack the protective skeleton of their parents. They go through several molts during the course of their first few months. For each molt, they climb out of their old skin, as shown here, and often eat it as a source of nutrition. They are constantly eating anything available—so when a long period with no food confronts them, they are able to survive adequately.

Cockroaches are strictly nocturnal, rarely seen during the day. Other night creatures such as centipedes, geckos, cats, and spiders are some of their natural enemies, who will crunch through their hard skin if they can catch the fast-running roaches.

*There must be limits to change. After all, we've had these same
old body plans for half a billion years.*
Rudolf Raff, developmental biologist, Indiana University

On a golden autumn afternoon in 1820, Robert Gibbon Johnson, a young colonel in the U.S. Army, stunned the people of Salem, New Jersey. He stood on the steps of the town's courthouse, and with a crowd gathered before him, he committed what seemed at the time a suicidal act: He ate a tomato.

John Postlethwait and Janet Hopson in *The Nature of Life*

The **tomato** (*Lycopersicon esculentum*) belongs to a family of poisonous plants, including the deadly nightshade and mandrake. Until recent history most people considered tomatoes as deadly as arsenic.

"*. . . And to help speed that enlightened day, to help dispel the tall tales, the fantastic fables that you have been hearing about the thing, to show you that it is not poisonous, that it will not strike you dead, I am going to eat one right now!*" Colonel Gibbon Johnson said as he ate a tomato for the first time in front of a crowd, many of whom were screaming and fainting at his daring spectacle. Colonel Johnson ate the tomato, didn't die, and was eventually elected mayor of the town.

Garlic (*Allium sativum*) is a member of the lily family. Its healing abilities have been recognized since at least 1500 B.C., to increase energy, as a sexual stimulant, to relieve inflammation, and to treat a long list of other ailments, including gangrene, digestive discomfort, and high blood pressure.

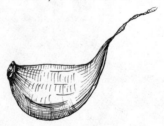

Garlic contains *allicin*, considered a more powerful antibiotic than *penicillin* or *tetracycline*. The delicate and pale flowers give no clue to the depth and substance of garlic's potential.

> *The humble garlic bulb, maligned for its powerful and lingering odour, is a*
> *wonderful medicine. As recognized centuries ago, it is an effective antibacterial,*
> *antifungal, antiviral, and antiparasitic remedy. . . . Garlic helps to restore*
> *wholeness and strength, imparts courage to help overcome fears,*
> *and increases resistance to parasitic entities and poisonous influences.*
> *Garlic has a stabilizing and harmonious effect.*
> Anne McIntyre in *Flower Power*

$\mathcal{A}$ member of the sunflower family, **Jerusalem artichokes** (*Helianthus tuberosus*) are very tall plants with typical yellow sunflowers growing on top.

Their name is a double mistake based on a misunderstanding started in the early 1600s by a French explorer. When Samuel de Champlain saw Native Americans eating the strange root of this sunflower, he and his staff ate them and said they tasted like artichokes, for lack of a better description. Years later, when the sunflowers had been exported to Europe, the Italians called them *girasole*, which means "turning toward the sun," as sunflowers do. The English then mispronounced *girasole* as "Jerusalem." Since then, no one has ever corrected the mistake.

We learn, as we say, by "trial and error." Why do we always say that?
Why not "trial and rightness" or "trial and triumph"? The old phrase puts it
that way because that is, in real life, the way it is done.
Lewis Thomas in *The Medusa and the Snail*

Some plants, such as the **wild potato** (*Solanum berthaultii*) have hairs on their leaves and stems that release a gooey substance when an insect steps on them.

Each hair is equipped with a gland that secretes the glue when triggered by a particular pressure—from an insect's legs, for example. The insect becomes stuck in the goo and eventually dies. Shown here is an aphid stuck on the wild potato leaf's glue; one gland is drawn greatly magnified to show detail. Cultivated potatoes don't have this defense mechanism.

There is a difference between a wild plant and a domesticated one. . . . Perhaps the easiest way to illustrate this is to think of the difference in feeling tone between a wolf and a domesticated dog, or of a mountain lion and the feel of a house cat. This same difference of feeling is also present in plant relations.
Stephen Harrod Buhner in *Sacred Plant Medicine*

The **yeast** used to make bread and beer is *Saccharomyces cerevisiae*, a live single-celled organism. It is the same as the fungus that grows on the surfaces of fruits and vegetables, as well as the dry powder sold in flat packages in the refrigerated section to make bakery products.

When mixed with water, yeast cells become active and begin "budding"—a small area of the yeast balloons out, then pinches off to create a new, identical version of itself. Yeast cells are dried into beadlike clusters for baking, and they can stay alive for up to six months.

Yeasts contain DNA instructions that allow them to make copies of themselves over and over as they continue to bud.

In 2020, you will be able to go into a drugstore,
have your [DNA] sequence read in an hour or so, and given back to
you on a compact disc so you can analyze it.
Walter Gilbert in *The Human Blueprint*, by Robert Shapiro

Amaranth (*Amaranthus*), also known as pigweed, grows wild along roads and in fields. Its importance as a food source is often overlooked or ignored, perhaps because it's just another inconspicuous weed. The nutritious seeds are eaten by birds and humans. Centuries ago, the Aztecs made a paste of ground amaranth seeds and shaped it into idols; these cookies were later eaten during rituals as a way of celebrating the spirit of nature. When the Spanish invaded, they banned growing amaranth so the Aztecs wouldn't be able to make the biscuits anymore, which they considered sacrilegious.

The patterns of communication that indigenous peoples created to communicate with these forces, they called ceremony. Of those patterns that were developed for relationship with Gaia, some are the ancient patterns of behavior that I call sacred plant medicine.
Stephen Harrod Buhner in *Sacred Plant Medicine*

Mushrooms are part of an enormous group of fungi. They are not always considered plants by scientists, because of their unplantlike behavior. The aboveground part of the mushroom commonly seen growing in yards, woods, and logs is short-lived, but the network of underground threads, *mycelium*, can live for centuries.

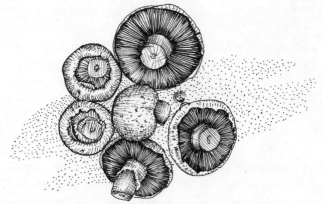

Mushrooms are carnivorous. They attack nematodes by releasing chemicals through their mycelium. Within seconds, the nematodes are paralyzed and are then digested by the mushroom.

Mushroom caps protect the delicate gills from being bombarded by raindrops. The gills need the moisture so they don't dry out, but the pressure from rain would destroy them.

In the speed with which they spring up, in their numbers, and in their strangeness, mushrooms are the offspring of the forest earth itself. One day the woods are dark, green, empty. Next morning they're full of pallid little visitors.
Castle Freeman, Jr., in *Spring Snow*

Wild turkeys (*Meleagris gallopavo*) are similar to domestic turkeys but thinner and with slightly different colors.

Male turkeys have an inspiring array of feathers with an iridescence and design worthy of comparison with any exotic bird—but for their *commonness*, they would be considered as impressive as eagles or falcons. However, the females—for whom their tails glow—are suitably impressed as the males strut to show off their good genes.

During courting, females choose males based partly on the male's ability to prove who he is—that is, by the effectiveness of his courtship signals. If she is confronted with several hundred males, which will she choose? The flashiest, loudest, cleverest, or biggest will be the one with the most to offer reproductively. Bright feathers and long, flowing tails indicate lack of parasites and good genes.

> *Doo lang doo lang doo lang . . .*
> *He's so fine. Wish he were mine.*
> *That handsome boy over there, the one with the wavy hair.*
> *I don't know how I'm gonna do it, but I'm gonna make him mine.*
> "He's So Fine" by Ronald Mack

Daddy longlegs (*Leiobunum*) are one of the most common creatures crawling around backyards, closets, trees, vacant lots, and woods.

What kind of animal are daddy longlegs? They have eight legs, so they're not insects; but they're not spiders, because they have only one body part and they don't spin silk. Their body shape is a clue that they are related to mites and ticks.

Daddy longlegs were once called harvestmen because farmers saw thousands of them during harvest moons and thought they were a sign of an abundant harvest. The full moon drives hundreds of species to cyclic activity, including mating.

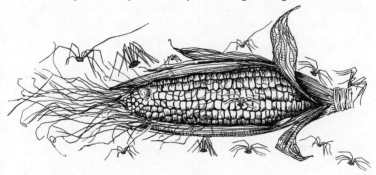

Nothing is more creative than nature, more evocative of creation
and the creative process, more a living metaphor of creativity. If we want to
learn, it is there to teach. But first we have to learn to look.
Dan Wakefield in *Creating from the Spirit*

*I*n the winter, decaying logs host populations of beetles, fireflies, centipedes, snails, frogs, spiders, salamanders, and **daddy long-legs.** Even if parent daddy longlegs die during the winter, their eggs hatch the following spring in the log's shelter. Each baby uses an "egg tooth" to break its way out of the egg. The egg tooth, which is similar to that of some reptiles and birds, disappears soon after hatching.

Very few predators attack daddy longlegs, even the babies, because of a scent gland in one of their legs that gives off a very disagreeable odor. Unwary birds have been seen wiping their beaks on the ground to get rid of the odor.

It is interesting to contemplate an entangled bank, clothed with plants of many kinds, with birds singing on the bushes, with various insects flitting about, and with worms crawling through the damp earth, and to reflect that these elaborately constructed forms, so different from each other, and dependent on each other in so complex a manner, have all been produced by laws acting around us . . . from so simple a beginning endless forms most beautiful and most wonderful have been, and are being, evolved.

Charles Darwin in *On the Origin of Species*

Deer mice (*Peromyscus*) are some of
the most widely distributed and successful mammals in North America.
Like other mice, they are nocturnal
and active throughout the year. Many
species have evolved to fit into niches of
different habitats, such as Florida's old-
field mouse, shown here. Its tiny, pale
body blends in easily with Florida's sandy
soil.

They stay in social groups of a
dozen or more, huddling during the day in logs, trees, and
burrows. These mice reproduce several times a year, creating
nests for their young from any available material.

The nests of rodents show far less variety than those of
birds . . . and almost any convenient material may be used. . . . One
mouse of my acquaintance created grave catering problems when it
escaped into a well-stocked larder and stripped all the
labels from food cans to make its nest.
Peter W. Hanney in *Rodents*

Memories of their animal envoys still must sleep, somehow, within us;
for they wake a little and stir when we venture into wilderness.
Joseph Campbell in *The Way of the Animal Powers*

*I*n nature, being "cute" promotes nurturing and protective feelings—the nonthreatening traits in cartoon
characters like Mickey Mouse are
those same features in baby animals
that create surges of tenderness.
Who could feel hostile or aggressive
toward a wide-eyed mouse or a
floppy-eared puppy? The "cuteness"
in the newborn **mice** shown here can only
help in their survival. By the time they mature,
they are still "cuter" than, say, rats. A human, faced with a rat or a
mouse, would probably react less fearfully and aggressively toward
the mouse.

Small children naturally develop plump, bulging cheeks, a large forehead, big eyes,
a small round chin, and, often, dimples. Just looking at them makes the heart
melt, and studies strongly suggest that such a response is biologically based. . . .
Cuteness triggers a protective response in both adults and children.
Diane Ackerman in *A Natural History of Love*

*U*sually more than two inches long, the caterpillars of the **Isabella tiger moth** (*Isia isabella*) are called woolly bears because of their "fur." The caterpillars are distinctively black at both ends, with reddish orange in the middle.

According to legend, the amount of black in the caterpillar's bristles is a sign of how severe the coming winter will be. Actually, the amount of black changes as the caterpillar matures, before the cooler weather stimulates it to seek a winter shelter.

In the early winter in the northern United States, the woolly bear is commonly seen crossing roads; in the South by this time of the year, the woolly bears are already mature, ready to take off in flight as yellow moths with peppery spots.

. . . We need to be willing to let our intuition guide us, and then be willing to follow that guidance directly and fearlessly.

Shakti Gawain

The more faithfully you listen to the voice within you, the better you will hear what is sounding outside. And only she who listens can speak.

Dag Hammarskjöld

At the beginning of winter, some insects enter homes to escape the cold. The familiar and nonstop chirping coming from a basement or closet is a sign that a **cricket** or two has come in for shelter. Immature crickets who stay outside in the winter usually die from the cold. Those who survive become active at the end of winter in search of food and mates.

Among the many chirps and calls of insects at night, most female crickets can distinguish the song of the male of their own species. Cricket songs are used to communicate territorial boundaries, danger, food sources, and mating needs.

Two men were walking along a crowded sidewalk in a downtown business area. Suddenly one exclaimed: "Listen to the lovely sound of the cricket." But the other could not hear. He asked his companion how he could detect the sound of a cricket amid the din of people and traffic. The first man, who was a zoologist, had trained himself to listen to the voices of nature. But he didn't explain. He simply took a coin out of his pocket and dropped it to the sidewalk, whereupon a dozen people began to look about them. "We hear," he said, "what we listen for."

Kermit L. Long, in *The Three Boxes of Life and How to Get Out of Them*, by Richard N. Bolles

*I*n 1995, Israeli scientists unexpectedly discovered that a deeply rooted temperamental trait of daring and restlessness comes from a gene dubbed the "novelty-seeking" gene.

Pine siskins (*Carduelis pinus*) are the novelty seekers of the bird world. They wander for most of the year in noisy flocks, often with large groups of other roaming birds. They have irregular migratory schedules and routes. Their drab colors give no clue to their impulsiveness and extravagance.

Their courting and mating behaviors are also enthusiastic. Several pairings may take place during a single breeding season. As soon as the chicks mature, parents leave to resume searching—for new territory, and to join with new flocks.

Everyone has some degree of novelty seeking—the only question is how much . . . people who score high are curious, impulsive, extravagant, enthusiastic, and disorderly. Low scores tend to be indifferent, reflective, frugal, orderly, and regimented. The difference is all in your mind; what you make of it is up to you.

Dean Hamer in *Living with Our Genes*

December 1

For a short time in the winter, migration stops and the sky is quiet and clear of traffic. Appearances and behaviors change as darkness, temperature, and barometric pressure increase. The arrival of winter profoundly influences animals on a cellular level—migration is over, food is scarce, daylight is short; a quiet acceptance settles through the woods.

Owls are one of the few creatures that actively move through the woods during winter nights. Searching the forest for nest sites months before nesting begins gives owls a chance to find abandoned hawk nests to use as their own.

Owls are the first to begin nesting. When food is scarce they lay few eggs or they don't breed at all. Guided by natural forces, owls eat what they need, sleep when they can, and mate according to their body's schedule. Their ability to thrive where other birds couldn't survive has made them a symbol of wisdom and authenticity.

December 2

A hawk who misses catching a rabbit does not try to become a weasel or raccoon . . . it hunts more intensely at the next opportunity.
Ted Andrews in *Animal-Speak*

The word *hawk* is from an old English word meaning "to seize." Hawks, with their sharp talons and powerful hooked beaks, are built for seizing animals. Mainly meat eaters, hawks can spot an animal from high in the sky, circle above it, and with target precision, swoop down to seize the meal and return to flight in one swift motion.

Competition for food is intense, even in rodent-rich woods. Typically hawks and owls share the same habitat, hunting for the same animals, but living together is tolerable—owls are night creatures and hawks are active by day.

Most hawks are large with wingspans over a yard, but some, like the **Cooper's hawk** (*Accipiter cooperii*), are only about the size of a crow. Their size makes them no less daunting hunters, however, and when searching for food to feed their nestlings, they seize any opportunity to attack, not returning until they have a furry or feathered package in their talons to bring to the nest.

Try? There is no try. There is only do or not do.
Yoda the Jedi warrior in *The Empire Strikes Back*

Rattlesnakes (*Crotalus*) are found throughout the United States and are easy to identify by the rattle at the end of their tail. The segments of the rattle are loose, and when the snakes are threatened, they shake their tail, creating a buzz as a warning to stay away. A rattler would rather scare away a trespasser than waste its precious venom by attacking.

Rattlesnakes, like all other pit vipers, have a sense organ that looks like a pit between the eye and nostril. All snakes with this facial pit are poisonous. The organ itself is used to locate warmblooded prey and can sense temperature changes far less than one degree.

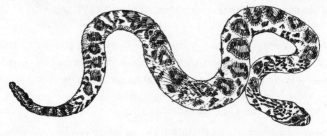

Walking away from a rattler is the safest way to avoid its bite, although our natural response is to freeze. Whether it's the sound of a rattlesnake's rattle or a bully's angry voice, we can't help but respond with a primal fear. Trying to control our primitive responses is as futile as trying to change the rhythm of our hearts.

Staring into the face of an angry rattlesnake is one of those things you are not supposed to do, and you know it. The thinking brain tells itself, "Why don't you get out of the way, fool?" while the primal brain resorts to a simple, "Aaagh!"
Natalie Angier in *The Beauty of the Beastly*

*P*it vipers, **rattlesnakes** included, breed less than once every three to five years. Hundreds of males may have to fight for days for the only fertile female in town. The winner, after courting with a contrasting gentleness, mates by locking himself into the female.

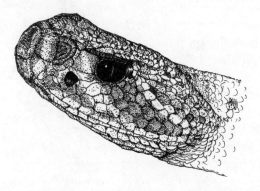

At no other time in nature's cycle is it more apparent than during mating that our drives, passions, and movements are controlled by a force beyond our understanding.

Following prairie rattlesnakes in Wyoming, scientists found that, during mating season, males embark each morning from their den on a grueling, five-mile round-trip search for willing females. And as they travel, they crawl in a line so straight it could have been penned by a draftsman. Should they have to deviate from their path to scoot around a pond or boulder, they return to the straight and narrow as soon as possible.
Natalie Angier in *The Beauty of the Beastly*

The **brown recluse** (*Loxosceles reclusa*) is also known as the violin spider because of the violin-shaped mark on its body.

The recluse is one of two extremely dangerous spiders in the United States, the other being the black widow. Even though they are small (less than half an inch) and nonaggressive, recluses defend themselves with a potent bite that leaves a painful wound. Within twenty-four to thirty-six hours, fever, chills, nausea, and joint pain set in. Small blisters around a swollen area are a sign of a recluse bite. The wound can take several months to heal.

Recluses often hide in dark secluded places—messy attics, basements, old logs, and unused closets. When stored blankets or towels are disturbed in trunks or drawers, a resident recluse responds by using her venomous fangs, particularly if the lives of her offspring are threatened.

Everything's got a moral, if you can only find it.
Lewis Carroll

*. . . Males are surprisingly reluctant to pursue interactions with women
unless they receive tacit encouragement with cues like eye contact. The two most
important signals in this respect are strong steady eye contact and the so-called
"coy" signal, in which eye contact is held for just a second, then followed
by a rapid look away accompanied by a slight smile or blush.*
Robin Dunbar in *Grooming, Gossip, and the Evolution of Language.*

*H*ard as it is to imagine, **silverfish** (*Lepisma saccharina*) couples engage in sensual and tender hours of foreplay: they approach each
other tentatively with quivering antennae, touching gently, then
moving apart in a slow-motion tango, then vibrating as they repeat
the process of touching and backing away—until the male is sure
that she will accept him. He then releases a thready package of
sperm near her and guides her on top of it. He positions her body
so that she becomes entangled in it and she accepts it, storing it
for later use.

*And the moment . . .
I can feel that . . .
you feel that way too . . .
Is when I fall in love
with you.*
"When I Fall in Love," by Edward Heyman
and Victor Young

To those who are awake, there is one ordered universe, whereas in sleep each person turns away from this world to one of his own.

Heraclitus

*E*ven though **mole crickets** (*Gryllotalpa*) spend most of their time underground in tunnels, they have strong wings and are powerful flyers. Their large forelegs dig through soil, and their husky bodies allow them to excavate long burrows.

They stay underground during the day and only come to the surface to feed at night. During mating, they fly toward bright lights. Their nocturnal habits are as biologically programmed as those of many other animals, including some humans.

Sleep researchers have recorded the depth of various dream activity in animals and humans. Prematurely interrupting this activity on a daily basis is as dangerous as turning off a car engine while driving seventy miles per hour on the freeway. Animals wake when they've finished sleeping, according to their own rhythm, not when an alarm clock buzzes.

Tasks that feel like climbing Mt. Everest when you're not alert can feel like a stroll around Walden Pond when you are. No one doubts that body clocks influence productivity. Their impact on bravery is less appreciated.

Ralph Keyes in *The Courage to Write*

Beavers (*Castor canadensis*) live in small communities by lakes and streams that are near food trees. One of the few animals that can change their environment, beavers control water levels and the shape of their surroundings.

Like most rodents, beavers have large incisor teeth in both jaws. "Rodent" comes from the Latin *rodere*, meaning "to gnaw." These incisors grow throughout their life and stay sharp enough to cut through tough timber or fine grass.

Females and males look about the same. The male's testes lie hidden in an abdominal cavity so it's impossible to tell the difference visually.

Both have sharply clawed front feet to dig and long fingers to grasp food and branches firmly. Their webbed back feet work like paddles to let them swim easily through water, while using their strong, flat tail as a rudder.

To understand Beaver medicine, you might take a look at the power of working and attaining a sense of achievement. In building a dream, teamwork is necessary. To accomplish a goal with others involves working with the group mind. . . . Each partner in the project honors the talents and abilities of the others. . . .
Jamie Sams and David Carson in *Medicine Cards*

I have learned silence from the talkative; tolerance from the intolerant and kindness from the unkind. I should not be ungrateful to those teachers.
Kahlil Gibran

*I*n the winter, **beavers** eat cuttings that they stored underwater in the spring, to add to their staple winter food of tree bark.

The kits, born in the spring, stay close to home for the first two years, learning and building their communication skills.

Communication among beavers is complex and sophisticated. Their "words" are scents made from the molecules of pheromones. Specialized glands produce fifty different chemicals; the subtle combinations of these pheromones give beavers the ability to communicate at least as many messages as humans can with twenty-six alphabet letters.

Pity us, the long, tall upright ones, whose sense of smell has weakened over time. . . . What are we missing? Just imagine the stereophonic world of aromas we must pass through, like sleepwalkers without headphones.
Diane Ackerman in *A Natural History of the Senses*

*Stings require stingers, and in the bees, ants, and wasps, stingers are highly
modified ovipositors (egg-laying tubes) that have evolved into syringes for
injecting venom into creatures that have caused offense. All of which means that
stingers and the ability to sting are a females-only phenomenon in the
Hymenoptera [bees, wasps, etc.] . . . which may make males largely irrelevant
in the nest-defending societies of their sisters and mates.*

John Alcock in *In a Desert Garden*

*B*ees and wasps both have stingers, but a wasp can use her stinger
many times; a bee stings once and then dies.

Mud daubers (*Sceliphron*), black and yellow wasps with long,
thin waists, are known for their nests of mud made
on walls, trees, soffits, logs, windows, or
under rocks. Females use their heavy jaws
to form mud balls into tubes placed side
by side as their nest. When the nest is
complete, she fills each cell with a
paralyzed spider body, then lays an
egg on each spider. She closes off
the cell before leaving her family to
develop on their own. A new generation emerges in the spring.

*. . . Freed from this responsibility and evidently unburdened by
stinger envy, male Hymenoptera attend to their own agenda, which
revolves around copulation rather than indiscriminately
educating predators and innocent bystanders.*

John Alcock in *In a Desert Garden*

Unlike the solitary mud daubers, **paper wasps**
(*Polistes*) are social. Females work together to
build nests made from wood pulp mixed
with their saliva. Eggs develop inside the
nests and females tend to the eggs until
the larvae pupate.

The wasps that emerge from the
first eggs are all sterile females who
remain with the nest to help the
queen tend her eggs. By the end of the
summer, eggs develop into females *and*
males, and the social structure of the nest
changes. Mating activities resume.

Fertilized females are usually the only
ones to survive the fall and winter. In the
spring, the surviving sisters gather material
from fibers and wood in a communal effort to
build new nests, creations worthy of the finest pot-
ters and paper makers.

*Art today is a very deliberate act. I feel, however, that art comes
from a deeper source somewhere—it's part of the act of just living:
you know, let's put on the beans and get the clay out.*
"The Sense of Process," by Rina Swentzell,
in *All Roads Are Good: Native Voices on Life and Culture*

If we believe that birds enjoy and suffer somewhat as we do, we have stronger motives for protecting them. . . . We feel more comfortable in a world enlivened by beings akin to us in mind, as in anatomy and physiology, than in one in which we are lonely exceptions. Our whole attitude toward life, our religion in the profoundest sense of the word, is subtly colored by our worldview.
Alexander F. Skutch in *The Minds of Birds*

The range of the winter migration for **tree sparrows** (*Spizella arborea*) depends more on weather than food. During mild winters, fewer migrants from Alaska and northern Canada are seen in their southern range. Tree sparrows are commonly seen in loose flocks hopping around on snow-covered fields and roadsides during mild winters. Often their breeding and winter ranges overlap.

Despite their name, tree sparrows spend a lot of time on the ground. Even nests are built low, among bushes and thickets. Nest building is a loose affair of available twigs and grasses, lined with feathers. Tree sparrow nests are more casual than those of most other songbirds, but with a strength and order that holds the female and her chicks securely.

How many birds do you know that when they've finished a busy few hours of nest-building, will tell themselves, "I can't stop now, I've got to build three more nests, or build this nest three times as big as the next sparrow's, to establish myself as the really successful sparrow on the block"?
Wayne Dyer in *The Sky's the Limit*

December 13

A Robin Redbreast in a cage
Puts all Heaven in a Rage.
William Blake

*A*merican **robins** (*Turdus migratorius*) are known as American generalists because they have as broad a niche as any bird, living as easily in urban areas as in thick woods throughout North America. They eat worms and insects, but can adapt to berries and fruits when worms aren't available.

Large flocks of robins gather in fields to forage, but smaller, less noticeable groups often arrive in their nesting areas in early winter. Lower temperatures and food scarcity prompt robins to migrate. But even when winter conditions are mild, they still journey south—sometimes it seems that they simply want a vacation. Robins in New Jersey head south to Maryland while Maryland robins shift down a little to Georgia, and so on. Robins seen in Delaware in October may not be the same ones from the week before, who have moved on for better food.

One of the hallmarks of our species is our ability not only to adapt to our environment, but also to change the environment to better suit us. We withstand the cold reasonably well, but we don't let its extremes bully us into migrating; we just build shelters and wear clothes.
Diane Ackerman in *A Natural History of the Senses*

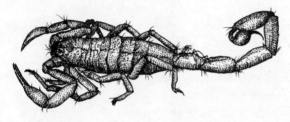

Scorpions (*Centruroides*) use their front pincers to grab prey, usually insects or spiders, then use their venom-filled stinger to paralyze them. Not aggressive unless provoked, they stay hidden under rocks, logs, or in burrows by day and emerge at night to forage for food. Some, like the desert scorpion shown here, can survive for months without water and for a year without food.

Scorpions give birth to several dozen perfectly formed minia-ture scorpions after a yearlong pregnancy. The babies cling to their mother through their infancy, going through several molts before mature enough to venture out on their own. Scorpions mature after about five years, much later than most other small animals.

If somebody were to put together a Guinness of invertebrates,
scorpions would merit multiple entries. They are some of the biggest, meanest,
longest-lived, most sensitive, most maternal, least fraternal, slowest, quickest,
and most luminous creatures among the arachnids and insects.

Natalie Angier in *The Beauty of the Beastly*

In a restless world like this is . . .
Love has ended before it's begun,
and too many moonlight kisses
seem to cool in the warmth of the sun . . .
"When I Fall in Love" by Edward Heyman and Victor Young

$\mathcal{A}$ long courtship between male and female **scorpions** starts with the female leaving a trail of pheromones to help the male find her. Highly sensitive organs in the male, called pectens, pick up the slightest trace of her scent.

Once they find each other, the male and female circle each other with their tails up while the male clasps the female with his pincers. They walk backward and forward in a sensuous tango that lasts for hours. In a tangle of tails, claws, and legs, she eventually accepts him as a mate. He drops a sperm package and maneuvers her until she takes it into her body.

Their nocturnal courtship ends by daylight, when the female, no longer needing his services, often eats him, head first.

It's too late to worry about your hair when you are about to lose your head.
Russian proverb

Carolina wrens (*Thryothorus ludovicianus*) are one of the little brown jobs unnoticed in backyards until they begin nesting in mailboxes, tin cans, gardening shoes, or discarded Christmas wreaths.

Carolina wrens do not migrate, even though northern winters bring cold temperatures that the little birds can't tolerate. Many freeze to death or die from lack of available food.

In an experiment, during an abnormally cold period one January, Carolina wrens had food provided to them on alternate days. The cold had been greeted by a silence among the wrens, but when one of them was provided with food, it began to sing. Not only that, when it began to sing, its neighbors stopped foraging altogether. So the moral is "if you've got it, flaunt it . . . and you may get more." And the upshot is that the rich do get richer.

Jake Page and Eugene S. Morton in *Animal Talk*

Violets smell like burnt sugar cubes that have been dipped in lemon and velvet.
Diane Ackerman in *A Natural History of the Senses*

*H*igh in vitamins A and C, the leaves and flowers of **common blue violets** (*Viola papilionacea*) can be eaten. Candy is often made from the flowers and used to decorate cakes, plates, and salads.

Their species name, Latin for "like a butter-fly," came from the flower's "wings." The lower petal is longer than the rest of the flower, to be used as a landing dock for insects; the two petals next to the landing surface are bearded, to comb pollen from visiting insects. "Blind violets" are produced by unpollinated flowers. These are self-pollinated and usually produce large quantities of seeds.

The other feature of earthly life that impresses us is its luxuriant diversity:
as measured by estimates of species numbers, there are some tens
of millions of different ways of making a living.
Richard Dawkins in *River Out of Eden*

*Those interested in perpetuating present conditions are always in
tears about the marvelous past that is about to disappear, without having
so much as a smile for the young future.*
Simone de Beauvoir

The plump bright berries of **holly** (*Ilex*) symbolize life in the darkness of winter. Centuries ago it was planted in neighborhoods to protect homes from evil, poison, and lightning.

Native Americans used a certain species of holly (*Ilex vomitoria*), shown here, to make a ceremonial tea; drinking large amounts of the strong brew would cleanse them by purging their systems of unwanted impurities.

*Holly is for people who are full of hatred, jealousy, envy, thoughts of revenge,
and resentment . . . Holly helps us to release those emotions, and to be
able to experience love toward others and within ourselves.*
Anne McIntyre in *Flower Power*

*I*nsects need wings to travel, but **fleas,** who have no wings, use a device that allows them to move around just as well. A structure that was used as a hinge for their ancestors' wings is now used as a spring mechanism. Why did fleas lose their wings in the first place? Maneuvering quickly between hairs was difficult enough without wings getting in their way—so the wings disappeared and more appropriate jumping skills evolved.

Thousands of species of fleas live throughout the world, and most have adapted themselves to exist on mammals: dogs, cats, rats, humans. Each species has a body specifically suited for its host, but all have bristles on a hard armored body that is extraordinarily flat, as if someone squashed them paper-thin so they could squeeze through fur.

Their flat bodies allow them to work their way through hair, and their bristles help them cling to their host, even during scratching and combing.

A complex mechanism triggers the explosive release of resilin energy that hurls the flea upward. Blasting off, the flea experiences an acceleration of 140 g's, 50 times that of the space shuttle after lift-off. . . . Aloft, it may cartwheel end over end, seemingly out of control. No problem: its six extended legs, covered with bristles and tipped with hooks, act as grappling irons to snag onto fur or leather.
Nicole Duplaix in "Fleas: The Lethal Leapers"

Catnip (*Nepeta cataria*) grows easily just about anywhere in North America, including gardens, houses, and city lots. White and pink flowers bloom on hairy stems that can grow up to a yard tall.

Catnip has been used for centuries to brew tea to calm nerves, soothe stomachs, and get rid of tension headaches.

The chemical in catnip (nepetalactone) that excites cats is the same substance that repels insects. Thus, the plant produces its own protection against harmful insects while inviting cats that may crush it in their ecstatic rolling. Interestingly, rats hate the plant; the French typically grow it with the herbs they cultivate for seasoning.

The kind of garden you maintain (vegetable, herbal, etc.) and the kind of animal life that visits it can be very insightful. It can often reflect how well you are consciously using your innate creative energies and abilities.

Ted Andrews in *Animal-Speak*

*Between the lion and the **lapcat** the feline family resemblance is unmistakable.
Cloaked in elegant camouflage and lethally armed, cats reveal what
British veterinarian David Taylor calls the essence of the perfect, polished
warrior.... The cult of the cat spans human history and geography.... We are
awestruck in the presence of the perfect predator—the emblem of power
and death. In the jungle—and everywhere else—the lion and his tribe are king.*

Cathy Newman in "Cats: Nature's Masterwork,"

National Geographic, June 1997

*God is really only another artist.
He invented the giraffe, the elephant, and the cat.
He has no real style. He just goes on trying other things.*

Pablo Picasso

*The **cat**'s mind is not thinking about how much money he needs,
or whom to write a postcard when he visits Florence: he is watching the mouse
or the marble rolling across the floor or the light reflecting in crystal.
He is ready with all of him to pounce.*
Natalie Goldberg in *Writing Down the Bones*

*Animals have the gift of living in the moment. They inhabit their physical
world with attention and grace. Taking a cue from their presence,
I learn the lesson of attention.*
Julia Cameron in *Blessings*

Several species of mice evolved to fit into different available habitats. The most familiar to humans is the **house mouse** (*Mus musculus*). Harems of females live and reproduce in territories controlled by one male.

Male house mice, much more aggressive and dominating than we usually observe, will kill some infants to gain control of female harems. By killing the infants of a previous harem master, the usurper removes his competitor's genes. In addition, the mother becomes ready to reproduce sooner.

A strange female represents an additional opportunity for the male to pass on his genes. Thus, males become more sexually active in the presence of new females, whereas a resident male's response to his familiar harem of pregnant mates is just the opposite. Having already inseminated these females, there is little or nothing to be gained by copulating with them again until they can rear new litters.

John Alcock in *Animal Behavior*

December 24

A territorial male lives with his harem and becomes habituated to his pregnant females (for obvious adaptive reasons) but it is quick to respond sexually to a new addition to his group. Moreover, although the harem master may find his pregnant mates sexually neutral, other males that happen to contact them do not treat them in this fashion.

John Alcock in *Animal Behavior*

Baby, baby I'm aware of where you go
each time you leave my door
I watch you walkin' down the street
knowing your other love you'll meet.
Haven't I been good to you?
Stop. Stop. Stop in the name of love . . .
"Stop in the Name of Love" by Lamont Dozier,
Brian Holland, and Edward Holland

ℳistletoe (*Phoradendron*) grows on large host trees, typically oaks, poplars, and several evergreens. The tangled and colorful little plant uses the nutrients from the host trees for its own growth. Its berries are covered with a poisonous sticky substance, toxic to humans but harmless to birds. Cedar waxwings eat the berries, then wipe the sticky juice off their beaks onto branches, where a new plant may grow.

A Scandinavian story about mistletoe tells about the god of peace who was killed by an arrow made of mistletoe. He was later resurrected and returned to health by the goddess of love. From this came the custom to kiss under a cluster of mistletoe to show that the plant was an emblem of love, not hate.

Mistletoe is recommended for people experiencing a period of rapid change and transformation in their lives. It gives one the strength and energy to surmount all the difficulties as the language of flowers tells us, and is a bringer of love and goodwill.
Anne McIntyre in *Flower Power*

Mistletoe has been associated with more myths and legends than almost any other plant. Because of the relationship with other trees, and its bright winter berries, it has become a symbol of shared aspirations, unity, and fertility. Our custom of kissing under the mistletoe may have come from these symbolic connections.

One seventeenth-century story claims that mistletoe was forbidden in church decorations because of its poisonous nature. Somehow Christmas traditions included secretly hanging mistletoe from doorways, under which kisses could be stolen. The original tradition requires that for each kiss, a berry should be picked and discarded; when the berries were gone, kissing stops.

> *There is a strong and powerful life force that moves within the bodies of the wild plants. But I saw that—in spite of the work human beings had done in the genetic development of plants species—what they have created does not carry that life force as strongly. I wonder now, as I did then, how is it that we have come to accept this dilution of life force in what we create as a normal thing?*
> Stephen Harrod Buhner in *Sacred Plant Medicine*

Redstarts (*Setophaga ruticilla*) are one of the most abundant birds in North America and definitely one of the brightest—in color, song, and body gestures. Known for their extravagant talent shows, males strut all their best stuff, including their songs, in the intense competition for females.

A female, who typically stays with the same mate for life, may reject her previous partner because his courtship qualities decline—her decision is motivated by her drive to breed successfully.

Males and females maintain separate (although close) winter territories, but during the spring mating season, males "brag" about their territory by using their vocal strengths to convince a female that it's worth her while to join him. By singing loud, long, and clear, he's letting her know that he has all the time and endurance in the world to sing for her—his property has plenty of food that kept him healthy in the past, and he has plenty left for her.

. . . Once having recognized a male of her species, the female may attend to the male's overall song output—the amount of singing he does over time—as a "true" advertisement of the quality of his territory. If it's a lousy territory, he'll be too busy hunting for scraps of food to spend much time singing.
Jake Page and Eugene S. Morton in *Animal Talk*

*E*astern chipmunks (*Tamias striatus*) spend most of their time on the ground during the day and underground at night, unlike squirrels, whose days and nights are lived in and near trees.

Chipmunks eat almost anything: nuts, berries, insects, baby birds, snakes, frogs, slugs, and mushrooms. They use their cheek pouches to carry food to their burrows.

Within their complex burrows are pantries specially created to store bushels of food for cold months, when they are in a semi-hibernation state. Their genus name, *Tamias,* is Greek for "one who stores and provides food."

Weasels, slinky enough to squeeze through the narrow burrow openings, are chipmunks' main predators.

*It's a different kind of world to grow up in when you're out in the forest
with the little chipmunks and the great owls. All these things are around you as
presences, representing forces and powers and magical abilities of life that
are not yours and yet are all part of life, and that opens it out to you.
Then you find it echoing in yourself because you are nature.*
Joseph Campbell in *The Power of Myth*

Weasels (*Mustela*) form a large group of carnivores ranging from a two-ounce least weasel to the sixty-pound wolverine. A mink is simply a water-dwelling weasel.

The weasel shown here, the long-tailed weasel, has a long, thin body that can squeeze into tight places when chasing small rodents.

The weasel is graceful, solitary and very silent. Though weasel people may often be loners, they uncover a lot about people in their lives. Their ability for silence enables them to go unseen and unheard, even in the company of others. . . . In the Native American tradition, the weasel has the medicine for seeking out secrets. Trust your own senses in regard to other people, and you will come out all right, even if it means going alone.

Ted Andrews in *Animal-Speak*

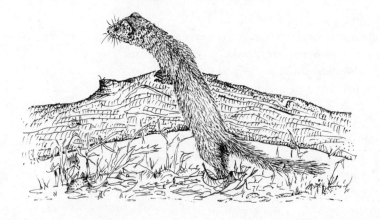

If you watch other animals and don't see pieces of yourself in their behaviors,
then you're not quite human, are you?
Natalie Angier in *Woman: An Intimate Geography*

Weasels will eat just about anything, including small mammals, birds, lizards, frogs, and poultry. Their "weasel" reputation may have come from their habit of sneaking into coops and killing chickens in a frenzy without eating them. Their normally shy, elusive nature doesn't deter them from these break-ins, nor from taking over other animals' burrows.

With billions of years of evolution embedded in every cell of every body, who knows what ancient forces prompt a creature to wander alone at night while another sleeps through the night content to be surrounded by family? When we dig into the soul of our cells, it's easy to see that philosophy, religion, and science are not separate at all.

We may prefer to view our behavior in psychological terms, but its origins are
biological, both in the individual and in the evolution of the species.
Myron Hofer in *The Roots of Human Behavior*

Things that matter most must never be at the mercy of things that matter least.
Johann Wolfgang von Goethe

River otters (*Lutra canadensis*) live along rivers and streams throughout North America. They have a language ranging from soft friendly chuckles to loud calls for food. They snarl, but only when threatened. When frightened, their shrill screams can be heard for a mile.

During the December to April mating, both sexes are compelled to wander. When they form a pair, they stay together for part of the year, but when the female is ready to give birth in the spring, she drives the male away.

Mothers are protective of the newborns, not even allowing the father to come near them for the first few months. When the pups are old enough to learn to dive, swim, and hunt, the father resumes an active role in parenting.

All our progress is an unfolding. . . . You have first an instinct, then an opinion, then a knowledge, as the plant has root, bud, and fruit. Trust the instinct to the end, though you can render no reason.
Ralph Waldo Emerson

ABOUT THE AUTHOR

A former senior editor at the Johns Hopkins University/ Applied Physics Laboratory at Cape Canaveral, CATHIE KATZ is now writing wildlife books in Melbourne Beach, Florida. She has lived in Israel, Holland, Germany, Spain, and Portugal, studying a broad range of natural habitats. She is the author of *The Nature of Florida* series, founder of the *Drifting Seed* newsletter with Dr. Charles R. Gunn, and director of an annual International Beachcombers' Symposium. She is currently writing *Ocean Spirit*, an illustrated book about the behaviors of ocean animals to show that science and spirit are inseparable.